Trust Within Global Virtual Teams

Trust Within Global Virtual Teams

Antecedents, Facilitators, and Sustainability Factors

Olivier Chavaren

iUniverse, Inc.
New York Lincoln Shanghai

Trust Within Global Virtual Teams
Antecedents, Facilitators, and Sustainability Factors

iUniverse, Inc.

For information address:
iUniverse, Inc.
2021 Pine Lake Road, Suite 100
Lincoln, NE 68512
www.iuniverse.com

ISBN: 0-595-27577-X

Printed in the United States of America

ACKNOWLEDGMENTS

I am deeply appreciative of the unswerving support I received from my wife not only during the writing of this dissertation but throughout the undertaking of this 'tough' Masters in Business Administration. Therefore, I want to dedicate this dissertation to my wife for her continual encouragement and the patience and love she so generously showered upon me in times of great difficulty, when I was managing both my work and study load.

More specifically, my thanks go to my tutor, Dr. John Sillince, for kindly supervising and guiding me through my dissertation. I am also grateful to him for suggesting the title of this dissertation.

Many thanks to the three heavy burdened project managers of a large global telecom company who provided me with an extremely useful hands-on insight. They will know who they are.

Special thanks are also due to the staff of the computer centre of Royal Holloway / University of London. Chris Horton guided me to the right person and always provided me with valuable responses to my technical queries. Special thanks also to Dr. Paul Pal, for contributing his time and effort especially with regards to the application of the SPSS software programme in the survey analysis. Thanks to Phil Taylor for creating and running the 'anonymiser' tool, which enabled the responses to arrive via anonymous e-mail, thus strengthening both number and quality of the responses obtained.

Last, but not least, I am grateful to three additional people. Firstly, *Chevalier* Paul Connoly, K.S.G. and Mr Dennis Di Mauro must be thanked for their support with regards to general editing. Secondly, Stephen Coates, Fellow of the British Institute for Personal Development (IPD), must also be quoted here for the time he granted me to clarify avenues in team relationships.

They have contributed significantly to the successful making of this dissertation.

May God always bless you.

Note to the reader: this empirical study contains both a quantitative aspect (the building of a model) and a qualitative approach (the practical view of international project managers).

PREFACE

The reason I accepted to write this preface is that I am convinced that relationships of Trust present a corporate challenge for worldwide organizations not only on a management level but also regarding the costs incurred if breach of trust occurs.

Due to its presence in approximately 60 countries through some 140,000 people (employees and agents) around the world, the AXA Group faces the challenges inherent to *virtual teams* on a daily basis. Whilst this type of relationship exists between American entities and the Headquarters in Europe, I also would like to emphasize the global aspect that now has come local i.e. within the US boundaries owing to the multicultural society that now defines best the United States.

To put things into perspective, the AXA Group ranks among the world's leading insurers and financial services providers. The Group operates in both domestic and international markets: large international risks, assistance and reinsurance.

Responding to the current observed need to increased efficiencies for global operations, more and more companies like us are setting up virtual teams to address a wide range of tasks through computer-mediated communications (CMC) such as e-mail, teleconference or video-conference. Failure to show a proper style of management to these individuals working in remote places—sometimes far-flung countries—in a timely manner would cause organisations to experience de-motivation of employees, poor risk management and eventually a high turn-over…

Global organizations are the most vulnerable to this risk owing to the high dependence on CMC because of geographical spread and, resulting in lack of control. Furthermore, the interdependences among team members and the lack of body language implies that these teams operate with dissimilar constraints to those required by face-to-face meetings. In real terms, the virtual teams pose a significant risk not just to virtual team members but also to their Management. Many are ill-prepared to these specific context. Therefore, virtual teams necessitate an *ad hoc* management approach based on proper tools that Olivier details in the along his dissertation and that encapsulates as follows:

i) "Can an optimal management of these virtual teams add value for organizations?"
ii) "Does a model entailing to successful virtual teams exist?"
iii) "If so, is it easily transferable?"

Nicolas E. Lance,

Chief Operating Officer Northeast Division,
AXA Financial/US.

Contents

LIST OF APPENDICES

GLOSSARY OF TERMS

EMBA	Executive Master of Business Administration
IPD	Institute for Personal Development
K.S.G.	Knight of the Order of St Gregory the Great
df	Degree of Freedom (statistics)
Asymp.Sig. (2-sided)	Asymptotic Significance (2-tailed) Level
Cross-tab	Cross-Tabulation
C.I.	Confidence Interval
X^2 value	Chi-Square Value

Trust

"confidence in or reliance on some quality or attribute of a person or thing, or the truth of a statement;
accepting or giving credit to without investigation or evidence;
giving credence to, believing (a statement); relying upon the veracity or evidence of (a person, etc.);
confident expectations of something; and
the quality of being trustworthy; fidelity, reliability, loyalty, trustiness."
(source: Oxford English Dictionary)

CHAPTER I

Introduction

The globalisation process (Dickens, P., 1997) of organisations linked with the rapid spread of the Internet and telecommuting has played a role in the rising number of teams inside and amid organizations. Virtual teams are clusters of people employed in common tasks or goals corresponding through electronic means, which can be electronic mail (e-mail), telephone or voice-mail, Web-based exchanges, video and/or audio, but in general having extensive relations online (Warkentin & Beranek, 1999).

1.1.   Outline of the problematic

Furst *et al* claim that, so far, companies do not manage their virtual teams with a singular procedure that could differentiate the type of management used from the one performed in their collocated teams. Although significant idiosyncrasies have been posited between virtual and collocated teams, both managers & researchers "ignore these differences at their own peril "
Jarvenpaa *et al (1998)* have already touched upon some aspects of the trust in virtual teams. However, some realms remain in the shade. This thesis would like to focus on the types of tasks, of individuals, team size & the length of project duration that are most suited for virtual collaboration and the sustainability of trust i.e.:
> *How to develop Trust in Global Virtual Teams?*
Antecedents, facilitators & sustainability factors.

1.2   Why it is important?

1.2.1   Theoretically

Trust is a significant input to many forms of exchange (Doney, Cannon, Mullen; 1998). Between firms' relationships, researchers demonstrated the role of trust in lowering transaction costs associated within uncertain settings (Dore, 1983; Noordevier, John, & Nevin, 1990) thus, enabling a firm to strengthen its competitive advantage (Barney & Hansen, 1994). Furthermore, trust is a valuable contributor to long-range connection or kinship betweens companies (Ganesan, 1994; Ring & Van de Ven, 1992), and is a signficant feature to enable successful strategic alliances (Browning, Beyer, & Shetler, 1995; Gulatti,

1995). Inside companies, trust enhances an effective achievement of the strategy, a better organization of the management (McAllister, 1995) and efficient team work (Lawler, 1992).

Therefore an appropriate approach of the issue of trust within organisation's virtual teams may provide a framework that can heighten the success of virtual teams. To achieve this, the following concepts needs to be defined:
  • what are the antecedents of trust & how to recognize them
  • what are the intrisic characteristics of a global virtual team

1.2.2　Empirically

Despite a growing enthusiasm for teams, little empirical research has been done to explore dynamics inherent in the virtual work environment (Watson-Fritz *et al*, 1998)

1.3　How to approach it?

As trust is a key component of the success of a virtual team, we will draw upon the different frameworks used to encapsulate the notion of trust in face-to-face relationships to single out the criteria that may be valid in global virtual teams.

Doney *et al* attribute the trust building process to 5 different pathways.

Trust may be formed via:
• a calculative process based on behaviour control
• a prediction process based on consistency
• an intentionality process based on common value and beliefs
• a capability assessment relying on competence
• a reliable network of strong connections enabling transfer from one party to the other.

Jarvenpaa *et al* posited a model of trust—called 'swift trust'—in a global virtual team based on the trustor's perceived ability, benevolence, integrity and the trustee's propensity to trust. 'Swift trust is a form of depersonalised action' that is highly correlated to virtual team productivity.

Mayer *et al* emphasise one another model of trust whereby 'team members will live up to their colleagues expectations'. Meyerson, Weick & Kramer demonstrated that virtual teams were associated with 'less emphasis on feeling, commitment, and exchange, and more on action and heavy absorption in the task'.

1.4   Methods

1.4.1   Research

A survey (a questionnaire including 39 questions) was conducted targeting 109 employees with responsibilities in large global companies. These primary data enabled us to test the propositions empirically.

1.4.2   Analysis

The questionnaire results were processed through a statistics software (SPSS 9.0).
This investigation was carried out by applying a range of quantitative methods such as frequencies and cross-tabulations.

1.5   Conclusion

Lipnack & Stamps stress the need for improved trusting relationships in virtual teams. Positive & high trust relationships are 'even more important in virtual teams' since the lack of daily face-to-face contact may result in some misunderstanding. They imply that for virtual teams, "trust has to substitute for hierarchical and bureaucratic controls". Therefore, for an organisation, it heightens the necessity to build balanced virtual teams that will provide efficiency over time.

CHAPTER II

The Trust Paradigm

Introduction on the Concept of Trust

2.1   A Cross-Disciplines Perspective

CHAP. III   THEORY CHAPTER

Lewicki *et al* (1995) envisage trust as an underpinning for social order that covers many academic fields and spheres of study. Appreciating why individuals trust, in addition to how that trust models community interactions, has been a fundamental focal point for psychologists (Deutsch, 1962; Worchel, 1979), sociologists (Gambetta, 1988), political scientists (Barber, 1983), economists (Axelrod, 1984), anthropologists (Ekeh, 1974), and scholars of organizational behaviour (Kramer and Tyler, 1996). Academics have seen trust as a central component in the wholesome character (Erikson, 1968; Shaver and Hazan, 1994), as a basis for social relations (Rempel, Holmes, and Zanna, 1985), as an underpinning for collaboration (Barnard, 1938; Blau, 1964), and as the foundation for constancy in social organization and mercantile exchanges (Arrow, 1974; Williamson, 1975; Zucker, 1986). For Sheppard and Sherman, academics have studied many aspects of confidence construction in such distinct realms as 'anthropology, economics, organizational behaviour, psychology, and sociology'.
Rousseau *et al* lay the emphasis on the special dissimilarities typifying conventional handlings of trust. He considers that intrinsic disagreements and conflicting premises are operating (Fichman, 1997). Economists are apt to perceive trust as either a computational process (Williamson, 1993) or as institutionally embedded (North, 1990). Psychologists frequently structure their evaluation of trust in idioms such as characteristics of 'trustors and trustees' and concentrate on an array of inner knowledge that individual characteristics produce (Rotter, 1967; Tyler, 1990; see Deutsch, 1962, for an instance of more computational approach by a psychologist). Sociologists frequently locate confidence in social traits of exchanges among individuals (Granovetter, 1985) or institutions (Zucker, 1986).

2.1.1   Foundations of Trust

Lately, academics of trust within firms have concentrated on appreciating the effectiveness of trust and attempting to shed light on how it comes about (Hosmer, 1995; Kramer and Tyler, 1996; Mayer, Davis, and Schoorman, 1995; Sitkin and Roth, 1993). Lewicki *et al* are more than ever recognising the doubt, intricacy, and changeability that is associated with the current high-speed worldwide corporate setting (D'Aveni, 1994; Hamel and Prahalad, 1994) and the ensuing key influence of confidence and mistrust within a competitive environment. Knowing the demands for swiftness (Eisenhardt and Tabrizi, 1995) and excellence (Schneider and Bowen, 1995), harmonized action in core projects (such as quality enhancement, consumer assistance, and novel manufactured goods improvement) has proved to be indispensable. Besides, owing to the competitive situations of companies, global changes, and development through key partnerships, the aptitude to efficiently expand and maintain key accords and bonds amongst contestants (Hamel and Prahalad, 1994) and within numerous nations and foreign language exchanges (Cox and Tung, 1997) has grown to be a vital skill. In each of these areas, the trusting intrinsic worth of the relationships between members—via multi-occupational groups, provisional partners, strategic alliances, and partnerships—are vital for thriving co-operation (Sheppard, 1995).

Trust-Building Process	Primary Base Discipline	Underlying Behavorial Assupmtions
Calculative: Trustor calculates the costs and rewards of a target acting in an untrustworthy way.	**Economics** (Dasgupta, 1988; Williamson, 1985)	Individuals are opportunistic and seek to maximize self-interest.
Prediction: Trustor develops confidence that a target's behavior can be predicted.	**Social psychology** (Deutsch, 1960; Lewicki & Bunker, 1995)	Individual behavior is consistent and predictable.
Intentionality: Trustor evaluates a target's motivations.	**Social psychology** (Rempel & Holmes, 1986)	Individuals are geared towards others, as opposed to themselves (e.g., motivated to seek joint goal)
Capability: Trustor assesses a target's ability to fulfill his or her promises.	**Sociology** (Barber, 1983; Butler & Cantrell, 1984)	Individuals differ in their competence, ability, and/or expertise and, thus, the ability to deliver on their promises.
Transference: Trustor draws on proof sources from which trust is transferred to a target.	**Sociology** (Granovetter, 1985; Strub & Priest, 1976)	Individuals and institutions can be trusted ; connections in a network are strong and reliable.

Source: Academy of Management Journal—Missippi State—1998

Table 1: **Building Processes, Base Disciplines and Underlying Behavioural Assumptions**

2.1.2 Three Core Economic Theories

Several authors envisage trust with disbelief; the concept of trust as not viable or as incurring unreasonable threat has been central to much literature in 'agency theory' (Eisenhardt, 1989; Fama and Jensen, 1983; Gomez-Mejia and Balkin, 1992; Harrison and Harrell, 1993; Hill and Jones, 1992; Jensen and Meckling, 1976), 'transaction cost economics' (Bromiley and Cummings, 1995; Gambetta, 1988; Ring and Van de Ven, 1989; Williamson, 1981, 1985), and 'game theory' (Deutsch and Krauss, 1960; Kramer and Brewer, 1984, 1986; Luce and Raiffa, 1957; Murnighan, 1991). Although others regard trust as a normal and critical factor of human exchanges (e.g., Gabarro, 1978; Rempel, Holmes, and Zanna, 1985), the three aforementioned theories appear to be the most relevant premises associated with the study of trust within an economic context. In agency language this supervision by workers curbs the "risk of opportunism" on the part of the supervisor and fosters the probability of positive results for the worker.

2.2   A Behavioural Approach

Recent research concentrates on conduct (Hosmer, 1995; Mayer et al., 1995), where confidence is identified as one contributor's positive hope of the conduct of another, when the contributor must decide how to behave (under constraints of defencelessness and reliance; (Hosmer, 1995), and as "the willingness of a party to be vulnerable to the actions of another party based on the expectation that the other party will perform a particular action important to the trustor, irrespective of the ability to monitor or control that other party" (Mayer *et al.*, 1995: 712).

2.2.1 Trust vs. Distrust

Lewicki *et al* focus on defining the boundaries of trust and distrust. Studies on trust within outfits have been available for over four decades. In initial studies academics linked confidence and mistrust to individuals' manifestation of trust in others intentions and motivations (Deutsch, 1958, 1960; Mellinger, 1956; Read, 1962). Mellinger, for example, encapsulated trust as a person's confidence in another individual's intentions and motives, and the genuineness of that individual's promise. Read (1962) developed on Mellinger's appreciation of confidence, considering that trusting people assumes their concerns to be secured and enhanced by those they trust, being loyal about revealing harmful private facts, being guaranteed of comprehensive data imparting, and are ready to overlook slight violations of the trust behaviour. Deutsch (1960) perceived trust as a person's belief in the intents and abilities of an exchange associate and the confidence that an exchange associate would act as expected. By the same token, Deutsch saw mistrust as an expectation of an exchange generating an unwanted conduct, arising from acquaintance with the person's skills and objectives. In mutual terminologies, academics regard mistrust as the expectation that counterparts will behave in a selfish fashion, still embarking on likely harmful conduct (Govier, 1994), and the assumption that able and reasonable conduct from particular people will not occur (Barber, 1983). Therefore, mistrust is seen as the reverse of confidence, and trust and distrust are appreciated through the conduct prism, with modest notice paid to the beliefs, intents, and motivations that support 'trusting/distrusting' and 'trustworthy/ untrustworthy' conduct.

In their research, Lewicki *et al* describe confidence in the terms of likely favourable prospects *vis-à-vis* another's behaviour, and mistrust as unfavourable prospects. They employ the idiom "another's conduct" in a very specific, but all-embracing fashion, broaching another's expressions, deeds, and choices. By "confident positive expectations," these researchers indicate a conviction in, a predisposition to ascribe honourable intents to, and a readiness to behave on the ground of another's behaviour. On the contrary, by "confident negative expectations," they signify a fear of, a predisposition to ascribe ominous intents to, and a wish to cushion oneself from the consequences of third party's behaviour. The aforementioned authors declare that both confidence and mistrust entail advances towards increasing clarity: trust pertaining to prospects of outcomes hoped for and mistrust relating to prospects of outcomes feared. They make the point that confidence and mistrust are discrete but related concepts. Furthermore, these researchers suggest that confidence and mistrust are not conflicting results of a specific range. There are components that contribute to the ebb and flow of trust, and there are attributes that contribute to the rise and fall of mistrust. These components mature and expand in the course of a person's familiarity with a third party in the diverse features of a human relationship. Even if widespread deductions across the connections may arise, it is likely for participants to both trust and distrust each another, according to the varying familiarity with the different features of intricate social relationships.

To summarize, Rousseau *et* al (1993) claim that there is no hitherto unanimously admitted academic meaning of trust. Yet, scholars concur that trust is essential in a variety of ways: it makes possible mutually supportive conduct (Gambetta, 1988); props up human interactions within a set of connections (Miles and Snow, 1992); curbs detrimental conflict; lessens transaction costs; permits the swift construction of efficient project teams (Meyerson, Weick, and Kramer, 1996); and enhances the successful resolution of disagreements.

Chapter III

Theory & Propositions

Antecedents of Trust

3.1   Hypotheses

3.1.1   Context

The main objective of this study is to examine the attributes that enable trust to emerge and be sustained within a global virtual team. Since the trend is to move to ever more globalised companies, the proliferation of these international remote groups is inevitable and with this proliferation, a key question arises which is directly related to the stated objective. After a deeper reflection, the objective is further translated into a meaningful practical form stated hereafter:

i) "Can an optimal management of these virtual teams add value for organisations?"
ii) "Does a model entailing to successful virtual teams exist?"
iii) "If so, is it easily transferable?"

3.1.2   Null hypothesis

The approach to this investigation was based on the traditional methodology of 'sampling statistics'. This is based on the idea of 'null hypothesis' (H_O), which in general terms is the hypothesis of no difference between the questionnaire variables under study. The null hypothesis specific to this survey is: 'There is no difference (or bias) to be expected between the range of options expressed by the candidates (Likert scale) and their socio-economic background.

3.1.3   Independent & dependent variables

Hereafter, ten attributes of trust are being discussed which consist of three independent variables and seven dependent variables. Reference to the relevant question of the survey is also indicated between brackets.

A/ Independent variables

I/ INSTITUTIONAL FACTORS (question Q3)

3.2   Perspectives on trust

This brief literature review of concepts of trust in economic, social, and organisation theory contemplates how divergent conceptual schools envision the societal settings and the role of trust. A dissimilarity among definitions of trust centred on a'calculative' process, an identification attitude and a knowledge approach has revealed the diverse premises relating to individuals and civilization. In addition, it has underscored the background-reliance of types of trust, primarily as some clues of the various understandings for initiating and prolonging trust in distinct social settings.

3.2.1   The formal trust (known as 'System trust')

The belief of formal or 'system trust' initially emerged in the production of Simmel (1964) and was granted meticulous improvement by Luhmann (1979) and Giddens (1990). Since civilization seems to grow more complex, it is likely to drop its assumed informality, whilst at the same time, the need for organising and 'determining the future'—and thus for confidence—turn out to be more vital (Luhmann, 1979, 20). Luhmann expands his view of 'system trust' through the concept of widespread vehicles of exchange—'money, truth, and political power'. The conceptual root of this type of confidence rests in that 'each trusts on the assumption that others trust' (Luhmann, 1979:75). In Giddens' production 'time-space distanciation' is overtly associated with the course of internationalisation and social disintegration (Giddens, 1990:21)

3.2.2   The Societal trust

It can relate to three options:
  • a concept of beliefs/pattern-rooted trust, envisaging a society as a community of common interest and values
  • institutional dispositions at a mid-scale and comprehensive tier
  • linked to the notion of 'system trust', it refers to faith in particular vital theoretical societal main beliefs or systems.

3.2.3   The 'social capital' of trust

With respect to Fukuyama (1995), he appreciates mankind as a sum of cultural organizations, and views trust as 'the expectation that arises within a community of regular, honest, and co-operative behaviour, based on commonly shared norms, on the part of other members of the community'. The occurrence of trust in the community culminates in 'social capital', a concept hired from Coleman

(1990). Fukuyama alleges that civilizations are different from each other to the degree in which trust permeates the entire nation, instead of staying restricted to relatives, tribes, or adjacent acquaintances. Besides he calls attention to societal trust that is difficult to expand scientifically. It is implicit that it is problematic, if not unattainable, to swap from a 'low-trust to a high-trust society'. Should the "culturalist" perspective that concentrates merely on the mid-scale tier be substituted by an institutional one, it would embrace the collective bodies (i.e. institutions) at an overall level. Zucker (1986) believes that institutional structures which generate confidence are numerous and diverse, and her examination deduces that they can be deliberately created.

3.3   Institutional-based trust

According to Lane (1998), institutional-based trust is linked to a distant type of confidence associated with strict societal constructs, which 'generalize beyond a given transaction and beyond specific sets of exchange partners'. Trust turns out to be an ingredient of the 'external world known in common' i.e. it evolves into institutionalised trust (Zucker, 1986: 63). Therefore, a quasi-legal framework restricts the threat to trust and gives rise to a more straightforward type of trust.

3.3.1   The *Vorleistung* or the previous pledge

Luhmann, Simmel, and Blau (1964), consider trust as a central cog of each interface scheme. Bar, 'the problem of time and knowledge', trust commands a previous pledge (*Vorleistung*). Consequently, trust needs to be complemented by instruments, which confine the danger of lost trust. Luhmann holds corpus juris as one such system of 'legal arrangements, which lend special assurance to particular expectations and make them sanctionable' (Luhmann 1979:34). Laws are perceived as dissuading or inhibiting cheating, nevertheless it is noteworthy to recognize that they perform simply as backdrop arrangements which confer self-confidence and which are not set in motion. The real employment of lawful penalties, for Luhmann, as for the majority of social researchers, is irreconcilable with a trust kinship.

Thus,

> PROPOSITION 1
> Within a virtual team, the higher the degree of trust in institutions, the greater the opportunity for trust to be established.

II/ DEPENDENCE ON OTHERS (question Q4)

3.4 Intrinsic features of trust taxonomies

Pearce and Bigley note that on several occasions academics have set forth the concept of vulnerability precisely inside their trust taxonomies (e.g., Mayer, Davis, and Schoorman, 1995; Mishra, 1996; Sabel, 1993; Zand, 1972). For instance, Mayer *et al* proposed that confidence is "the willingness of a party to be vulnerable to the actions of another party based on the expectation that the other will perform a particular action important to the trustor, irrespective of the ability to monitor or control that other party" (1995: 712). Sabel utilizes the notion of defencelessness (i.e. vulnerability) in a fairly different fashion: "Trust is the mutual confidence that no party to an exchange will exploit the other's vulnerability" (1993: 1133).

3.4.1 Vulnerability: a sine-qua-non condition for trust to emerge

Pearce and Bigley refer to the writings of Mishra (1996), which draws on Moorman, Zaltman, and Deshpande (1992) to mention that, in the absence of vulnerability, the notion of trust is not required, as outcomes do not affect trustors. Kee and Knox (1970) propose that the analysis of trust includes contexts in which an individual has an essential factor at risk and is aware of the likely untrustworthiness and hurt from the other. By the same token, Gambetta asserts "for trust to be relevant, there must be the possibility of exit, betrayal, defection" (1988: 217). Equally, Coleman suggests that trust settings are these "in which the risk one takes depends on the performance of another actor" (1990: 91), and Granovetter (1985) insists that the intrinsic personality of trust offers the option for the trustee to behave dishonestly. In addition, many researchers on organizations who have endeavoured to appreciate how mercantile exchanges appear to be structured (e.g., Bradach and Eccles, 1989; Bromiley and Cummings, 1995; Chiles and McMacklin, 1996; Cummings and Bromiley, 1996; Granovetter, 1985; Nooteboom, 1996; Nooteboom, Berger, and Noorderhaven, 1997; Ring, 1996; Ring and Van de Ven, 1992; Zaheer and Venkatraman, 1995) regard trust as an instrument that alleviates the threat of untrustworthy conduct between those involved in a wide range of business dealings.

3.4.2 Common exposure

Considered as a whole, the studies on the theme of trust are grounded on the common notion that performers (e.g. the team members) turn out be, in some respect, mutually exposed as they act together in a societal context, human interaction, or systems. Trust has been deemed as an appropriate label for a variety of paradigms used to comprehend dissimilar occurrences linked to the concern of performer vulnerability. Therefore, this intereliance entails the participants embarking upon actions. Thereby, they catalyse upon the force of their team to head towards forecasted milestones achieving their ultimate intent: the co-success of the project.

Thus,

PROPOSITION 2
Within a global virtual team, the higher the dependence on other team members, the more the fertile ground for trust to emerge.

III/ PROPENSITY to TRUST (question Q11)

3.5   Absorption of mistrust

With regard to intrinsic models of trust, Pearce and Bigley posit that features are present within people that prompt them to trust or be suspicious *vis-à-vis* others with whom they are not familiar. The core questions for these kinds of theories revolve around the issues of how people extend their predisposition to trust and how these preferences influence their beliefs and deeds (e.g., Hardin, 1993; Rotter, 1967, 1971, 1980). Rotter's study on trust is viewed as emblematic of this school and appeared to be among the most usually accepted and accredited contributions to organizational research on the subject. He hypothesizes that trust is a somewhat constant conviction centred on people's deduction from their initial years of practice. Next, he advocates that the intensity of trust's influence on conduct is closely linked with the contextual freshness that people tackle. For Rotter, as events happen to be ever more unknown to people, the impact that their trusting nature has on their actions matures. Put another way, as individuals grow to be more familiar with particular individuals, their own understanding of others is converted into the chief factor in their judgments and actions. Thus, this enables the individual to deal more efficiently with distrust.

3.6   The 'Multiplex-relationship' or the role of the third-party

Sheppard and Sherman shed light on the role played by the presence of others. In this perspective, one complex human interaction deserving debate is that emphasized by Sitkin and Roth (1993). These writers discovered that a lawful device for restoring breach of confidence frequently has the adverse consequence of producing distrust. This occurrence may possibly be best demonstrated in "multiplex relationships". When working together within an organization, economic vehicles enjoy a clearly dissimilar interaction with each other compared to situations when they interrelate through a go-between or "third-party". It is their interaction with the third party and, paradoxically, the prerequisite for institutional management on legal equality (such as appropriate procedure regulations) that generate coldness in the dyad. For instance, nations act in a different fashion in the presence of a great, powerful state. It is the influence of a prerogative (i.e. the 'authority') interaction on other mode of relationships that may generate aloofness. The "third party" can arrive to control the area.

3.7 Trust hints

3.7.1 Unit grouping

Since those who are classified as one are likely to enjoy common objectives and beliefs, they are apt to see each other in a constructive perspective (Kramer, Brewer, and Hanna, 1996). Therefore, one team member will be more prone to model trusting values *vis-à-vis* other team members. For instance, Zucker, Darby, Brewer, and Peng (1996) observed that being a part of the same outfit engendered the trust required for researchers to pool resources when conducting studies. In their research, Brewer and Silver (1978) noticed that individuals considered "in-group" associates to be more reliable than "out-group" associates. These researches offer confirmation that "unit grouping" rapidly leads to a high level of trusting values. As an illustration of the quick outcomes of "unit grouping", in predicting the success of a forthcoming meeting between a pair who had never previously met, Darley and Berscheid (1967) observed that the information that one would be matched with the other was apt to augment the one's regard for the other's attributes. Relating this to a novel assignment group, "unit grouping" would permit one member instantly to develop a trusting attitude towards another group associate.

3.7.2 Interactive effects.

Mc Knight *et al* suggest that "token control efforts" will act together with classification systems, confidence in humankind, and structural promise convictions, reinforcing a person's ability to develop trusting convictions. "Token control efforts" will offer an individual the delusion that his or her optimistic confidence in humankind can be relevant to the other member, by persuading themselves that he or she is harnessing ability—not merely luck—to a trust-associated assessment of the other person. Likewise, "token control efforts" will (1) create self-assurance that one's constructive classification of the other individual is accurate, and (2) strengthen the assurance that structural protection generates a safe atmosphere and, by a knock-on effect, that the person engaged is reliable. In the early exchange, "token control efforts" will reinforce the inclination of classification processes, trust in humankind, and a structural assurance conviction to generate a high degree of trusting convictions".

Thus,

> PROPOSITION 3
> Within a global virtual team, the higher the propensity to trust, the greater the favourable framework for trust is fostered.

B/ Dependent variables

I/ COMPETENCES (question Q6)

3.8   Field covered.

3.8.1   Definition

Competence or ability allude to the collection of aptitudes that permit a trustee to be appreciated as capable in some precise realm (Jarvenpaa *et al*, 1998).

3.8.2   Core role of competences in a trusting relationship

Additionally, apparent "ability" (Cook and Wall, 1980; Mayer *et al*, 1995; Sitkin and Roth, 1993) or its outcome—"competence" (Butler, 1991; Mishra, 1996)—can be fundamental attributes of trust. Lacking the assessment that one's supervisor holds the "competence" or "ability" to accomplish the executive responsibility, a worker is reluctant to build up trust in that supervisor. Even if neither of these assessments automatically prompts trust among supervisors and workers, each place a "perceptual" underpinning that fosters the probability that workers will respond optimistically to reliable conduct on the part of the supervisor.

3.9   Constraints

3.9.1   A time-consuming process

To appreciate honesty and aptitude, individuals need to appraise their counterparts on the basis of their prior record; in particular, other's marked evidence or existing achievement in a group. Consequently, this implies that, for honesty to be assessed highly, an individual must secure available knowledge on how consistently others reached their prior obligations and how strongly their execution corresponded to the expected objective standard of give-and-take. By the same token, to assess ability more highly, individuals may request comprehensive data on the other members' qualifications, job practice, and present organizational perspective. To appreciate goodwill, individual data have to be disclosed by others to reinforce commitments on mutual aspiration, gains, and appeal in setting up a superior human exchange.

3.9.2   Accuracy

According to Whitener *et al*, research psychologists categorize three attributes that impinge on assessment of "trustworthiness": (1) correct facts, (2) clarification of choices, and (3) sincerity. In numerous researches correctness in facts' has had the most convincing impact on "trust-in-supervisor" when evaluated alongside other attributes (e.g., "desire for interaction, summarization, gate keeping, and overload"; Mellinger, 1956; Muchinsky, 1977; O'Reilly, 1977; O'Reilly and Roberts, 1974, 1977; Roberts and O'Reilly, 1974a,b, 1979; Yeager, 1978). Subordinates regard supervisors as reliable when their message is precise and "forthcoming" (i.e. helpful).

As a matter of fact, the proficiency demonstrated *vis-à-vis* their counterparts by the team members heightens their self-confidence and eventually facilitates their relationship with third parties.

Thus,

> **PROPOSITION 4**
> Within a global virtual team, the higher the competences, the higher the probability for transference process (i.e. similarity) to occur.

II/ SIMILARITY (question Q8)

3.10   Transference process

Whitener *et al* make the point that two mental systems shape workers' understanding of white-collar "trustworthiness": (1) identified resemblance and (2) aptitudes. Here, we shall focus on the former attribute. Trust frequently develops between two individuals as they are interested in each other and observe that they have analogous features (e.g., Creed and Miles, 1996; Giffin, 1967; Larzelere and Huston, 1980; McAllister, 1995; Zucker, 1986).

3.11   Classification procedures

According to Mc Knight *et al*, classification procedures allow great degrees of trusting convictions. In a novel relation an individual can employ three kinds of classification procedures to cultivate trusting values: (1) "unit grouping", (2) stereotyping, and (3) "reputation categorization" "Unit grouping" implies placing the other individual in the identical cluster as oneself. "Stereotyping" signifies putting another individual into a broad class of people. "Reputation categorization" means that one assigns traits to another individual based on "second-hand information" about the individual. The former factor (1) has already been dealt with in the variable: 'propensity to trust' (Please refer to part A/ III/) and the latter attributes (3) were included in the feature: 'social interaction' (Please refer to part B/ VII/).

Typecasting ("Stereotyping") can be applied either to a general grouping, such as sex (e.g., Orbell, Dawes, and Schwartz-Shea, 1994), or on a more specific field, such as discrimination for or against professional groups (e.g., second hand car sales representatives). At their initial gathering, team members might outline "stereotypes" about each other, based on tone (e.g., masculine/feminine or native/overseas; Baldwin, 1992) or physical appearance (Dion, Berscheid, and Walster, 1972; Riker, 1971). Through an affirmative typecast, one can rapidly map out constructive trusting attitudes about the other by matching from the *ad hoc* group into which the individual was filed. In the early interaction, classification processes that place the other individual in a positive category will be likely to generate a superior degree of trusting convictions".

3.11.1 Illusions of Control Process

They are known as the interactive effects that increase trusting beliefs. Mc Knight *et al* describe why the delusion of "control process" will act together with classification procedure; confidence in humankind, and structural promise attitudes yield a high level of trusting convictions. Individuals in an unsure context will undertake few actions to attempt to reassure themselves that circumstances are under their own command (Langer, 1975). This leads to an idealistically overstated assessment of their own command (Taylor and Brown, 1988), which Langer labels "illusions of control." "Illusions", clearly, imply observations that diverge from reality, and extensive support validates the existence of "illusion" in mental procedure (e.g., Fiske and Taylor, 1984). The impression of a command system that facilitates the framing of a trusting conviction could be analogous to the system by which individuals turn out to be over-confident of their assessments, as conveyed by Langer and Paese and Sniezek (1991). Initially, one shapes a faltering conviction, and then one looks for hints that corroborate the conviction. Even without any indication, the effort of surveillance has a propensity to amplify an assurance in one's assessment (Davis and Kotteman, 1994). By the same token, even a minor exertion at validating one's faltering trusting conviction in another could increase one's assurance that a high level of trusting convictions is secured.

3.11.2 "Token Control efforts"

Individuals can make a preliminary effort to assess another individuals' reliability, otherwise they can, upon encountering an individual, straightaway try to determine whether or not they can sway that individual in a small way (e.g., make the person smile). Mc Knight *et al* named such actions "token control efforts." One person is not aiming at classifying the other but, instead, is assessing his or her aptitude to handle the other person fruitfully. At first, an individual is prone to employ "token control efforts" since she or he is not aware through prior experience whether or not the other has the characteristics required to be deemed reliable. Subsequent to performing such little efforts to check, the person may establish an unduly stark self-assurance that one's affirmative classification, confidence in humankind, and structural promise conviction are accurate and, thus, that the other individual is reliable. Langer for instance, in a research on "overconfidence", discovered that "token control efforts" increase one's probabilities in a draw (i.e., by selecting their personal lottery voucher) caused one to be very "over-confident" of succeeding.

Trust theorists have speculated that confidence creation comprises delusion (Holmes, 1991; Meyerson *et al*, 1996). The outcomes of one study of experiential trust research backs this stance. Kramer (1994) revealed that cogitating for a handful of seconds on others' reasons and objectives enhanced an individual's self-confidence in the correctness of his or her assessments of the others. Cognitive judgements are apt to enhance one's self-assurance because, as Langer observed, they transfer a task farther from the sphere of luck and nearer to the sphere of an ability-centred assessment. Thus, "token control efforts" can assist an individual's self-assurance in confidence-linked convictions.

Thus,

> **PROPOSITION 5**
> The more a team member perceives similarities in another member, the easier it is for the interpersonal skills to manifest themselves (leading to in depth team spirit).

III/ INTERPERSONAL SKILLS (question Q7)

3.12   Enthusiasm & smooth handling of the conflicts

In their research, Jarvenpaa *et al*, (Please refer to section B/ V/) lay the emphasis on the positive tone demonstrated by certain candidates. The high-trust individuals conveyed enthusiasm and overwhelmed others with praise and support. On numerous occasions, the high-trust groups stated how fortunate they were to enjoy such a good-running group. Still, at the conclusion, the partners endeavoured to praise each other for outstanding performance. Two of the high-trust groups were persuaded at the beginning of the task that they would be the successful group. The high-trust teams dealt with difference of opinion so smoothly that it was hardly noticeable that an argument had emerged. If a partner formulated a proposal with which another disagreed, the dissenting partner reacted not by straightforwardly tackling the argument but by proposing an option together with a clarification. The low-trust teams were deficient in optimistic attitude in their exchanges. Compared to the high-trust groups, the low-trust teams demonstrated little feeling of any type in their communication. Nor did the partners present any enthusiasm for winning a financial reward that was promised to the winners; the low-trust groups converged on what they may be deprived of if they act badly instead of what they may obtain if they work properly.

3.13   **Fundamental skills**

3.13.1 Time Management

The high-trust teams overtly broached the task agenda, ascertained milestones, supervised the milestones, and watched time carefully, reminding other individuals of the impending closing date. Besides, the high-trust teams were more alert to time zone discrepancies and how to deal with the worldwide clock to curb the time lags when nobody was performing on the allotted task. The low-trust teams did not discuss time management except for reminding others of the due final date. The low-trust teams only hinted at the time zone discrepancies in respect of who should present the finished assignments. The low-trust teams tended more to ask the supervisor for additional time. In a nutshell, the low-trust teams demonstrated neither a 'sense of urgency' from looming deadlines nor a conception of time control.

3.13.2 Team Building & Group personality

Fascinatingly, the high-trust teams did not spend much time on team methods, apart from one group in the initial sluggish phases. Instead of being worried that somebody else was tackling exactly the same task, team members on the high-trust teams attempted to generate high-quality achievement and then offer the assignment to the group for reaction and enhancement. The low-trust teams expended comparatively more time on processes as individuals attempted to avoid responsibility and persuade others to undertake the task.

Group training that concentrates on fostering knowledge communication among co-employees and promoting dedication and achieving of assignments ahead of time in the mutual procedure may be presumed to generate a superior appreciation of other co-employees' "ability, integrity, and benevolence", coupled with general team confidence. The impact on group trust is awaited since the training ought not simply to disclose knowledge on the individuals, but also to facilitate the construction of the group personality, which is a significant spur to confidence in a mutual situation. As a result, Jarvenpaa *et al* develop the following premise: 'The degree of involvement in the team-training will be strongly linked with the group trust as well as with other partners' identified aptitude, honesty, and goodwill. In addition, suitable clarification and well-timed responses on decisional choices lead to higher levels of trust (Folger and Konovsky, 1989; Konovsky and Cropanzano, 1991; Sapienza and Korsgaard, 1996). Obviously, supervisors who make themselves available to clarify their choices carefully are prone to be understood as reliable.

These authors point out that compared to the high-trust teams, the low trust teams demonstrated few social exchanges. Hitherto, in contrast to the high-trust teams, the low-trust teams seldom revealed understanding: what small feeling was shown was likely to mirror doubt in relation to whether anybody was perusing their e-mail, or irritation and dissatisfaction that no one else was contributing.

Thus,

PROPOSITION 6
Within a global virtual team, the higher the interpersonal skills, the higher the probability for integrity to be recognized.

IV/ INTEGRITY (question Q10)

3.14   Clarification

Trust in a pair interaction emerges from characteristics linking a trustee and a trustor. The trustee features are the person's appreciation of (1) ability, (2) goodwill, and (3) honesty. Ability has already been defined in the competence variable (Please refer to the variable 'competences', part B/ 1/). Goodwill or benevolence is the degree to which a trustee is thought to exhibit interpersonal attention, and the dedication to be helpful to the trustor further than a self-seeking motive. Integrity is commitment to a collection of main beliefs assumed to make the trustee trustworthy and reliable, to the trustor.

3.15   Intrinsic characteristics

3.15.1 Demonstration of Concern

Goodwill—exhibiting care for the well-being of others (Mayer *et al*, 1995, McAllister, 1995; Mishra, 1996)—is a component of a reliable conduct and encompasses three actions: (1) to exhibit importance and understanding of team members requirements and care, (2) to behave in a mode that integrates employees' interests, and (3) to avoid taking advantage of others for the sake of one's personal interests. These deeds on the part of supervisors can cause subordinates to recognize them as trustworthy and benevolent. Research has demonstrated such factors in executive trustworthiness to be a significant element that results in trust between tutor and protégés (Butler, 1991; Jennings, 1971).

3.15.1 Goodwill

In conventional exchanges, Mayer *et al* envisage that, over time, goodwill should augment. The exchanges will disclose knowledge *a propos* to the goodwill of the counterparts. A recent study on computer-based teams proposes that goodwill might predict team trust after the individuals have acted together for a while. Walther (1997) observed that collaborators who were physically separated, of differing backgrounds, and who were by no means permitted to convene face-to-face (i.e. who relied entirely on computer-based exchanges), shared further care and registered advanced stage of closeness, on top of collective and "physical attraction" communication, than did collaborators in the same venue. In an additional analysis, Walther did not observe computer-based exchanges teams to be more assignment-focused than head to head groups. Based on these analyses, Walther explained a "hyperpersonalization" model for teams confined to computer-mediated relations. The model contends that, since "individuating" knowledge (a signal that assists individuals to discern if they are alike or dissimilar, for instance, bodily) is so rare in a virtual situation, individuals presume resemblance and are inclined to divulge attributes and signals on others that aim at emphasizing this resemblance. Consequently, this over-reliance on resemblance can cultivate sharpening of concentration, attention, and a conviction in the value of a group interaction. For this reason, Jarvenpaa *et al* anticipate that over time, in an international virtual team, partners' appreciation of others' goodwill will have a greater impact on team trust.

3.16   Psychological contracts

3.16.1 Premises

Sheppard and Sherman elaborate on the "intentionality process" embedded in psychological contracts referring to an array of convictions between the trustor and the trustee. Their approach rests on Rousseau (1995), who considered the precursor of commitments in the light of cognitive agreements (namely 'psychological contracts') and their infringement. Essential to the analysis of these contracts is the premise that these 'agreements' are grounded on reciprocally understood requirements. Rousseau proposes that a number of elements discriminate 'psychological contracts' from other types of expectations within employment relationships. A crucial attribute of these contracts is that the person willingly consents to undertake specific pledges as they comprehend them (Farnsworth,1982). As asserted by Rousseau, "[A] contract is a mental model that people use to frame events such as promises, acceptance, and reliance" (1995: 27). Once moulded, assumed commitments are fairly long lasting and unwilling to change (Rousseau, 1995). While prospects merely hint at what the staff member anticipates obtaining from his or her supervisor (Wanous, 1977), psychological contracts allude to the noticeable reciprocal responsibilities that typify the worker-manager rapport. Since they encompass convictions in mutual and pledged commitment, psychological contracts can, when infringed, create mistrust, frustration, and the likely termination of the partnership (Argyris, 1960; Rousseau, 1989; Wanous, Poland, Premack, and Davis, 1992). Deviations from the stipulations undertaken in the contract classically breed intense antagonistic responses, such as sentiments of breach or treachery (Rousseau, 1989).

3.16.2 Reciprocity

For Zucker, trust hinges on prescribed, communally created and lawful arrangements, which secure trust. Trust is prone to surface when there is:
• reciprocity beyond team perimeters and therefore major social gaps among teams
• reciprocity throughout geographical space
• reciprocity linking a substantial number of mutually dependent, non-separable dealings

Together Zucker and Luhmann embrace the vision that the institutions (as exemplified in the variable 'institutional factors' in part A/ I/) lay the foundations or offer backings for confidence formation in a more multifaceted culture.

3.16.3 Psychological Contracts vs. Quadratic trust

Sheppard and Sherman claim that responses to psychological contract abuse stand for the most perceptive difference among them and Fiske (1990) and Rousseau (1989). Fundamental to 'quadratic trust' (i.e. trust within a team) is the notion of a group of people who jointly take steps to buttress the foundation of their interaction, whereas essential to a psychological contract is the array of convictions relating to the trustor's vision of the trustee's motivations. Many features could impact on these convictions, and strengthen trust both within and between groups. Yet, the point of responsibility is rather dissimilar in the two stances. One originates from a fraternity; the other is an attribute of the trustee's appreciation.

3.17　Face-to-face vs. virtual context

In a conventional head to head setting, trust requires time to grow. Cummings and Bromiley (1996) propose that group trust has an emotional, mental, and comportment/demeanour aim element. McAllister discovered that mentally established trust attributes are an antecedent to the growth of emotional-built trust. Mayer *et al* insist that, in the initial phases of an interaction, honesty/probity (or 'integrity') is more dominant than goodwill (or 'benevolence') to the construction of trust. Gauging benevolence necessitates data, which require time to collect. Despite the fact that Mayer *et al* do not label the precursors of 'ability, integrity, and benevolence' as *affective* attributes, they do correlate benevolence with the course of relationship development.

In a remote-team setting, Jarvenpaa *et al* anticipate honesty and aptitude to be especially convincing antecedents of trust since the setting is an impediment to human interaction development. In their research's perspective, team members were restricted to 'asynchronous' digital correspondence and to the sporadic employment of 'synchronous "chat" amenities. For Zack (1993), "the degree to which the mode of [electronic] communication allows participants to experience each other as being psychologically close" (p. 211) rests on the wealth of the prevailing collective interpretative background. This judgement was underpinned by Markus (1994) who ascertained that "lean" digital correspondence can be fertile in the context where the team members are familiar with each other, but if the members are restricted to digital exchanges over the long term, they expect their interaction to be "cold and impersonal" (p. 520). Among unfamiliar people who do not enjoy a mutual history and are new to each other's characters, there is no collective background. Consequently, digital exchanges can be presumed to be distant and assignment-oriented. Trust in a 'virtual-team' situation may therefore be more clearly associated with "ability and integrity, and less to benevolence". In the earlier phases, a worldwide virtual-team's trust is predicted more clearly by team members "assessment of the other individuals" honesty and aptitude than by the other members "benevolence".

Finally, sincere exchanges, in which supervisors communicate opinions and information in a responsible fashion with subordinates, enrich understanding of trust (Butler, 1991; Farris, Senner, and Butterfield, 1973; Gabarro, 1978; Hart, Capps, Cangemi, and Caillouet, 1986). The emphasis in exchanges is on imparting and sharing thoughts. This factor is more strongly linked to the first of the above factors that concentrates on delegation and the relinquishing of supervision. Yet, both factors build subordinates' trust in their supervisors.

Thus,

> **PROPOSITION 7**
> Within a global virtual team, the sooner team members display integrity/ benevolence, the sooner 'Swift Trust' is revealed.

V/ SWIFT TRUST (question Q5)

3.18   The work of Jarvenpaa et al

Jarvenpaa *et al* (1998) conducted a longitudinal study in which seventy-five teams consisting of 4 to 6 members residing in different countries interacted and worked together for 8 weeks. They eventually single out a dichotomy between two types of groups: the high-trust teams and the low-trust teams. The former seemed to exploit functions so that they were capable of restricting team interreliance to a reasonable level. The latter carved up the contributions so that they could get rid of their interreliance. The work undertaken by Jarvenpaa *et al* has to be considered for the understanding of virtual teams and the emergence of 'Swift Trust'. Therefore, his research, although not exhaustive, is regarded as authoritative on the subject, requires a wide coverage in accordance with the one given in this report.

3.18.1 A key attribute of virtual teams

This variable throws light on the realm of the virtual teams as opposed to face-to-face groups. According to Jarvenpaa *et al*, a virtual team consists of a provisional group of team partners who 'have never worked together and do not expect to work again' (21, p168).

3.18.2 A de-individualised behaviour: action first

Indeed, team members operating in a virtual environment do not have the scope to build up trust in an incremental and intensifying manner. Preferably, the team members perform as if confidence exists from the onset. While trust is classically theorised as both an emotional and a knowledge-based paradigm, *swift trust* is a type of de-individualised act. As Meyerson, Weick, and Kramer (1996) contended, "there is less emphasis on feeling, commitment, and exchange and more on action,…and heavy absorption in the task" (p. 191); "swift trust may be a by-product of a highly active, proactive, enthusiastic, generative style of action" (p. 180). The "swift trust" allows partners to be pro-active, and this activity will assist the parties to preserve trust and face indecision, vagueness, and fragility while toiling away at multifaceted inter-reliant duties with unfamiliar people in a context of intense pressure on time. In addition to the pro-active attitude, the other approaches connected with the high trust teams (Please refer to the aforementioned study of Jarvenpaa *et al*) appear to support the Meyerson *et al* 'survival' systems of momentary teams and consequently are related with *swift trust*. Meyerson *et al* examine how there are few exclusively social relations in provisional teams since "anything that subtracts from task performance…should be a glaring threat" (p. 177). Jarvenpaa *et al* observed that the international virtual teams were assignment-focused.

3.19   Factors that sway *Swift Trust*

3.19.1 Frequent interaction

Lastly, high degrees of interaction have a propensity to curb vagueness and uncertainty and ought to reinforce confidence in provisional teams. In the high-trust teams, individuals conversed regularly and offered widespread responses among them. The high-trust teams seemed to demonstrate swift trust from the onset. More specifically, the teams' initial written exchanges enclosed clues of proposals and confident activities. The low-trust teams did not reveal any explicit deficiency of trust at the outset; thus, Jarvenpaa *et al* suppose that confidence was present from the start as well in these teams. Yet, this confidence declined almost instantly, since the individuals were deficient in actions and proposals. Conversely, the achievement-focus in the high-trust teams brought about the strengthening of trust. Consequently, achievement appears to be a vital precursor as well as a consequence of trust. Actions that spread ahead of the title of the task reinforced trust. To recapitulate, Jarvenpaa *et al* maintain that 'trusting action is as much an antecedent of trust' as a product of it. The connection between 'action and trust' seems to be extremely "recursive" in a virtual team setting.

3.19.2 Handling of 'free-riders'

In his research, Jarvenpaa *et al* find that individuals in high-trust teams demonstrated initiative, spontaneously asked for responsibility, and fulfilled their promises. Moreover, the high-trust teams handled determinedly the so-called 'free riders'. The high-trust teams either gave prior notice of their forthcoming non-attendance or arranged a remote connection. The addition of further pressure strengthened the intensity of the appreciated dedication the individuals displayed *vis-à-vis* the team. Whilst the low-trust teams deliberately paid no heed to the free riders, the high-trust teams tackled these concerns by notifying the assignment manager of any inactive individuals. Albeit the teams were uninformed of the final results of their grievance—i.e. dropping out the inactive member or not from the task-, partners were more relaxed as a team since they pinpointed the individuals that were not contributing. This permitted the team to refocus on the committed partners. For the low-trust teams, it was the other way round. They underwent inertia, categorized by asking of questions but rarely supplying any material contribution, and by the request for assistance but hardly ever volunteering. The team members also seldom alerted the members prior to their absence.

3.19.3 Empathetic mode

Although the exchanges in the high-trust teams were assignment-focused, it is significant to mention that it was still sympathetic. The team members examined each others' assignments and outcomes in an extremely helpful and empathetic mode, which consequently strengthened the team's shared dedication and goodwill. Moreover, the awareness of restricted time-scale and overt time supervision is linked to Meyerson *et al*'s remark that "temporary teams rarely exhibit certain kinds of dysfunctional group dynamics" that contend with "jealousy, misunderstandings, and hurt feelings" (p. 190). For Meyerson *et al*, "there is simply not enough time for things to go wrong" (p. 190).

3.19.4 Task Goal Clarity

In his empirical research, Jarvenpaa *et al* exemplify how the high-trust teams debated the purpose of the task to a larger degree than the low-trust teams. In case of vagueness in the tasks, the individuals in the high-trust teams did not balk at getting in touch with the supervisor with queries prior to building their personal premises. As early as during the initial team training, the high-trust teams displayed familiarity with the tasks goals and disclosed their own objectives within the framework of the general cooperation and the tasks. By contrast, the low-trust teams had few discussions on assignment objectives. Even then, the majority of such exchanges merely dealt with an individual who was unclear as to what he had to achieve. Individuals of the low-trust teams did not reveal awareness of the tasks and did not commit their specific individual objectives to the tasks during the team training beyond assertions like "spend as little time as necessary."

To summarize, *Swift Trust* enables team members to feel more comfortable in the achievement of the task by showing their competences.

Thus,

> **PROPOSITION 8**
> Within a global virtual team, the faster the team espouse a 'full action strategy' (i.e. 'Swift Trust'), the easier the predictability to spring out.

VI/ PREDICTABILITY (question Q9)

3.20   Explicit expectations

Luhmann (1979) appears to propose a comprehensive theoretical examination of trust. He enlightens the concept of trust by relating it to the community purpose it achieves. For Luhmann, trust is an instrument by which performers lessen the intrinsic difficulty of their exchange process. They achieve it through the acceptance of explicit expectations regarding the impending actions of individuals by picking from among an array of alternatives. Trust soaks up intricacy to the extent that somebody who trusts behaves as if the trustee's conduct is predictable.

3.21   Behavioural attribute

3.21.1 Behavioural consistency

WHITENER *et al* assert that "behavioural consistency" (i.e., trustworthiness or expectedness) is a significant feature of trust (Butler, 1991; Gabarro, 1978; Jennings, 1971; Johnson-George and Swap, 1982; Robinson and Rousseau, 1994). Trust implies the readiness to be exposed to the behaviour of another individual and the readiness to take risks (Johnson-George and Swap, 1982; Mayer *et al*, 1995). If supervisors act consistently time after time, no matter the context, members of staff can anticipate the supervisor's potential actions more accurately, and their confidence in their ability to formulate such a forecast ought to augment. Furthermore, staff members turn out to be eager to engage in more risks in their involvement or in their interaction with their supervisors. Expected, constructive conduct strengthens the intensity of trust in the human relation (Graen and Uhl-Bien, 1995).

3.21.2 Behavioural consistency vs. behavioural integrity

Whitener *et al* detail their perception of behavioural integrity. Subordinates monitor the consistency between executives' language and actions and form an evaluation of their "integrity, honesty", and ethical nature. Dasgupta (1988) has recognized two actions—(1) saying the "truth" and (2) fulfilling pledges—as vital natural precursors to ascriptions (i.e. "attributions") of integrity: ascriptions that influence workers' trust in their supervisors (e.g., Butler, 1991; Gabarro, 1978; Giffin, 1967; Larzelere and Huston, 1980; Mayer *et al*, 1995; Ring and Van de Ven, 1992). Despite the fact that behavioural consistency and behavioural integrity have some resemblance, they are separate attributes. Both reproduce a consistency that lessens workers' apparent risk in trusting their supervisors. Yet, on the one hand, behavioural consistency echoes the trustworthiness or predictable ability of supervisors' actions, grounded on prior deeds. Behavioural integrity, on the other hand, hints at the consistency between what the supervisor says and how he or she acts. In a nutshell, the former lays the emphasis on the time attribute whilst the latter focuses on the subject.

3.22   Trustor's properties

Regarding the trustor properties, a predisposition to trust is a common individual attribute that express-es a widespread belief of how trusting ought to be. This attribute is supposed to be constant throughout the relationship as well as from one situation to another, and is swayed by a trustor's ethnic, societal, edu-cational practice, and by the nature of the person's character. Regarding the trustor characteristics *vis-à-vis* those of the trustee's, previous study has established that the trustee attributes shed more light on the differences in interpersonal trust than does the trustor's common capacity to trust.

Thus,

PROPOSITION 9
Within a global virtual team, the higher the predictability, the higher the ability to develop social interaction over time (through the reputation effect).

VII/ SOCIAL INTERACTION (question Q12)

3.23   Reputation effect

Mc KNIGHT *et al* emphasise the strength of "reputation categorization". Individuals with superior repute are classified as reliable people. Reputation can reflect occupational aptitudes (Barber, 1983; Powell, 1996) or the other trusting values: "benevolence" (Dasgupta, 1988), integrity, and prospective ability. An individual may be recognized as a capable person because she or he is a part of a capable team (Dasgupta) or because of this individual's performance. Thus, if the person has a good reputation, one will rapidly engage in trusting attitudes about that person, even without prior information.

3.24   Dyadic vs. Quadratic Trust

Trust in a team is more complex than dyadic trust (i.e. trust between pairs) since there are numerous trustees, each with dissimilar traits. Quadratic or collective trust, as identified by Cummings and Bromiley, is "a common belief among a group of individuals that another individual or group (a) makes good-faith efforts to behave in accordance with any commitments, (b) is honest in whatever negotia-tions preceded such commitments and (c) does not take excessive advantage of another even when the opportunity is available." Based on the writings about 'dyadic trust', Jarvenpaa *et al* investigate trust pre-cursors in a global virtual-team backdrop. Their paramount premise is that in a global virtual team,

team trust rests on other team members' identified aptitude, honesty, and goodwill, as well as of the partners own inclination to trust."

Lane proposes that system trust (Luhmann, 1979; Giddens, 1990), i.e. confidence in conceptual schemes such as the political system, diverges from money and truth in that it relates to theoretical societal attributes which enable a society to be more or less constant and predictable. The strength or vulnerability of such scheme trust will impact on the extent to which people are set to enlarge trust further than a core intimate assembly.

The same author asserts that within traditional exchanges, the development of trust arises in an incremental fashion and the extent of confidence granted is prolonged in very small stages. Team members progressively test whether the other member is reliable. The gradual development of trust necessitate that the intent of trust and the degree of threat associated are gradually amplified (Ring and Van De Ven, 1992:489). Child proposes that 'calculative trust' can turn into emotional-grounded trust (Child, 1998), or knowledge trust into benevolence trust (Sako, 1998). Sako's concept of a ranking of trust admirably condenses this conversion procedure.

It is also advocated that the procedure for constructing trust can be simplified if boundary-spanning partners in communication relationships have frequent individual exchanges (Bradach and Eccles, 1989), if inspection of the communication by a go-between is agreed, or if one-sided agreements—specific investments (Barney and Hansen, 1994), or pre promise—are established (Sako, 1998)

Thus,

> PROPOSITION 10
> Within a global virtual team, the higher the ability to interact socially through trustworthy principles, the greater are the chances to build a successful team and to sustain trust over time.

Chapter IV

Research Methodology

4.1   Selection of the Organisations

It was decided to send a direct questionnaire to the employees of two types of global organisations: the following large companies and corporate professional services or consultancies:

ENTITY	Type of company	
	Consultancy	Large Firm
EQUANT (France Telecom Group)		X
Alcatel		X
GTS—Global Tele System		X
Cisco System		X
Carrier One		X
Infonet (owned by KDD, KPN, Telefonica…)		X
WorldOnLine (Tiscali)		X
Hewlett Packard		X
Royal Dutch Shell		X
RVI (Volvo Trucks)		X
Materne (Hillsdown Holdings)		X
Solvay		X
Nokia		X
Krediet Bank Luxemburg		X
Hertz Lease (Hertz Group)		X
Appstech (ORACLE's consultants)	X	
Cap Gemini/Ernst and Young	X	
PriceWaterhouse-Coopers Lybrand	X	
Salustro-Reydel	X	

Table 2: **Typology of Companies' Respondents**

Respondents were primarily in the New Technology of Information and Communication (NTIC) sector (60%) i.e. they chiefly work in Telecom, IT or software companies. This trend is intrinsically related to one attribute of the very nature of the survey: computer-mediated-communication. Indeed, when surveying IT or Telecom companies, the chances are higher that they would use these new media they sell (telecom operators) or promote (IT organisations).

Main Country	Frequency	Percent	Cumulative Percent
FR	17	30.9	30.9
UK	13	23.6	54.5
USA	7	12.7	67.3
B	5	9.1	76.4
LUX	2	3.6	80.0
BRAZIL	2	3.6	83.6
JPN	2	3.6	87.3
Misc.	7	12.7	100.0
Total	55	100.0	

Table 3: Distribution of Respondents' Physical workplace (Q33)

Although responses arrived from the 5 continents, the total number of countries involved did not exceed 16 (Please refer to the appendix for further details). This is primarily due to the spreading of the businesses. However, more than a quarter (16.36%) of the respondents were based in a host country i.e. different from their homeland. This tends to highlight the fair degree of globalisation of the respondents. In addition, a relatively significant number of subjects (8.8 %) had two countries of residence. It means that they were also living in an additional nation for more than 40% of their time. This may be due to the fact that some multinational enterprises base their headquarters in two places.

4.2   Selection of the Candidates

4.2.1   A two-fold approach

Gaining access to employees with responsibilities within large companies was not a sinecure. These heavy burdened individuals are rather difficult to access, especially the senior top managers that require peace and quiet place in ivory towers. Therefore, the electronic media—i.e. e-mail—was selected to reach these executives directly, bypassing their assistants, and to obtain a swift feedback. As the topic was both personal and arduous, the sampling methodology relied to a great extent on a modest network of people, which ultimately generated the required amount of contacts. Therefore, the first step consisted in collecting the e-mail addresses of the future respondents and asking them to provide at least 5 additional addresses of potential respondents. From the 20 initial contacts, we then reached 109 contacts as some offered some extra contacts.

4.2.2   Sampling procedures

Throughout the study, the respondents were selected at random in line with sampling procedures, after applying eligibility criteria as required by the guidelines of the current research. The selection of the candidates themselves within the companies was based on a declarative attitude. If they responded positively when asked 'do you work in a virtual team?' a survey was submitted to them, provided that they agreed. Within the survey, several questions (e.g. Q21) cross-checked indirectly the presence of bias in the reponses i.e. whether the participants were actually part of a virtual team. This proved to be the case. All the surveys were sent from and received on a dedicated e-mail address namely trust-in-global-virtual-teams@voila.fr in order to heighten the professional handling of the study. Of the respondents, almost one tenth (9.09%) declared they would like to know the results. A follow-up is currently being processed.

The percentage of error to determine the minimum sample size has indicated a possible bias of 12% which indicates that the results may be over or under—evaluated by this figure.

The response rate indicated 50.5%, which is a moderate achievement considering the following elements. Dr Paul Pal, a statistical expert from Royal Holloway/ University of London, recommends sending 5 times more questionnaires (i.e. 'candidates') than the final required number (i.e. 'respondents'). This rule means that, generally speaking, only 1/5 will answer. In this case, to get 100 responses 500 surveys should have been sent. However, this rule relates to unknown people in a regular setting. Here, the survey was conducted towards semi-known people and within a corporate context. Whilst some candidates were still on holiday, others mentioned that they were facing restrictive time constraints. In particular, people working in finance departments had to focus on the month's end. Indeed, the main concern related to the high position of the candidates in the hierarchy with heavy schedules. More than half (58.2%) of the subjects belong to one of the three following categories Management, Senior

Management or Directorate. A respondent declined to fill in the survey asserting that it was "not related to [his] job description."

4.3   The questionnaire

4.3.1   An anonymous method

A structured questionnaire consisting of four pages (a total of 39 questions including 23 questions on the topic and some additional demographic characteristics questions) was administered via electronic mail and thus completed independently before being returned. To increase the response rate, the survey was introduced with a cover letter and the sentence: "Your name has been kindly suggested by (name of the original contact)…". As respondents belonged to a professional context and the topic—their personal views on trust—was quite engaging, the decision was made to run the questionnaire anonymously by the means of an 'anonymiser' created for the purpose of this study. This allowed respondents to state more freely their personal beliefs.

4.3.2   A behavioural perspective

Within the questionnaire, the emphasis was placed on the definition of the terms employed, below the question, to avoid any misunderstanding. (Please refer to the appendix for the coded questionnaire). Respondents had to mark or rank multiple-choice questions and statements, and were also offered the opportunity to formulate their personal response (i.e. 'other, please write in').As the survey was conducted within corporate organisations, the personal demographic attributes such as 'Income and occupation title' could not easily be asked. Therefore, the level of affluence is inferred from the educational background. Furthermore, the emphasis was on behavioural aspect i.e. 'what you do rather than what you think". (Please refer to the appendix for the main taxonomies of survey questions). Two taxonomies were created in order to encapsulate the qualitative answers of open questions about "the ideal characteristics of a super virtual team member" and of the hobbies as well.

4.3.3   Pilot test & follow-up

One pilot test of 5 interviews with the printed e-mail and survey was conducted. This allowed us to narrow down an 'average completion time' (15-20 minutes) and to remove technical words that would threaten non-native English speakers. The typography was also slightly heightened to facilitate direct reading onto the monitor of the computers. The e-mails—with the questionnaire as an attachment— (Please refer to the appendix) were sent on the 22nd of August 2000 indicating a time lapse of 10 workings days to return it. In addition, one response arrived after the deadline to be processed. A reminder had been sent to 30 people to draw their attention on the approaching deadline. However, the anonymous response system made it impractical to conduct a selective follow-up as we didn't know precisely who responded. Therefore, the follow-up process primarily focused on the nationalities we had not yet received. Five surveys arrived after the deadline and thus were not included in the analysis. Then, all the responses were transferred into numerical data in order to perform statistical analysis in SPSS.

4.4   Interpretation of the results

Two project directors and one project manager, working for a telecom company operating in 75 countries, were interviewed on the phone for 2 hours each. The three interviewed team managers were enjoying a team management experience of 10 to 15 years in a face-to-face context and at least 3 years in a virtual setting. The primary focus of the questions was the results of the survey and how to foster a trust atmosphere. Therefore, their expertise enables us to put the results of the survey into perspective.

4.5   Limitations of the research

Although one tenth of the participants—as already mentioned—demonstrated superior interest about the topicality of the survey, some appeared to be irritated by the subject or unable to participate due to time constraints. Whilst the first category manifest themselves via non anonymous e-mail sent to trust-in-global-virtual-teams@voila.fr (including comments and asking for feed-back about the final results), a Russian executive of the second category mentioned that was "not in my job description" and though it was a "joke".
Yet, one of the most salient limitations may be the language barrier. Although the pilot test together with the definition of the terms included in the survey attempted to ensure a clear understanding, 3 inquiries about the meaning of some words may highlight that this topic is rather tenuous to deal with in a foreign language.

Last, but not least, the sample population may be inherently tenuous to approach. Indeed, these management employees face an extremely heavy schedule: business trips, conference calls, video-conferences…This led to an increased rate of 'unable to contact' albeit a follow-up procedure was carried out. The number of respondents should reach a minimum of 100 individuals to ensure a lower error risk.

4.6   Future implications of the study

For research

Due to time constraints, certain aspects of this study were not investigated in details. It is therefore suggested that further investigations explores mistrust should be in more details focus as this study primarily laid the emphasis on trust. Furthermore, it is rather a new topic and the technology will still evolves. Therefore, new behaviour towards these "enablers" may be worth considering in a near future.

Chapter V

Results & Discussions

5.1   Quantitative Data Analysis

A summary of results of the survey is presented here. A number of useful findings emerged. More specifically, evidence was available to answer questions within a virtual setting on:

a) The influence of the 'institutional factors on the 'colleagues' trustworthiness/confidence (Q3).

b) The interdependence on other colleagues in order to achieve working goals (Q4).

c) The relative significance of action as soon as possible (i.e. 'swift trust') versus social exchanges (Q5).

d) The assessment of the competences of the team partners (Q6).

e) The appraisal of the level of 'interpersonal skills of the team partners (Q7).

f) The evaluation of the congruence of thinking and acting—when it comes to concrete things— between the respondents and their team partners (Q8).

g) The capacity to predict the action of my 'virtual' colleagues (Q9).

h) The recognition of display of good will—of the team partners—when interacting with each other. Q10.

i) The absorption of occasional acts of mistrust by others (Q11).

j) The ability—when relationships are strong and reliable—for trust to transfer from one person to another (through reputation effect) (Q12).

5.1.1   Procedure

Most of the organisations were selected among FORTUNE 500 global companies with operations in at least 60 countries and in compliance with the UNCTAD ranking for internationalisation. The sample was checked to ascertain that there was an unbiased and complete spectrum of companies according to age of the respondents and the size of the companies. From the selected sample, 55 respondents—from 17 firms—participated in the survey thus indicating a 50.5% response rate.

The data from the responses to the questionnaire were recorded onto the Data Editor of the SPSS application package to provide quantitative measurement with a view to further statistical analysis of mean calculations, cross referencing of data, and Chi-square statistics (i.e. for testing "goodness of fit") of the different variables. This quantitative representation was used to derive inferences related to trust within organisations. Tables were used extensively for the analysis; however, only the relevant ones will be displayed in this report.

5.1.2   Frequencies

In the survey, the core questions asked included question Q3, Q4,…Q12. Each of these questions had a number of levels of opinion scaled from 1-10 in line with the Likert scale. The frequency analysis of all these core questions is presented in the following tables and their histogram plots are included.

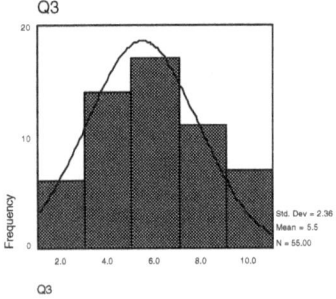

Q3: *In a virtual team, the perception of my colleagues' trustworthiness/confidence is influenced by 'institutional factors'.*
The levels of opinion are normally distributed around level 6.0 (moderate agreement)

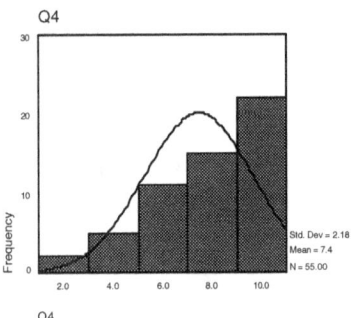

Q4: *In a virtual team, in order to achieve my working goals, I depend very much on other colleagues.*
The highest frequency is at level 10.0 (high agreement)

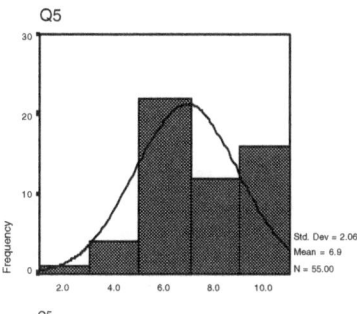

Q5: *In a virtual team, I usually concentrate on action as soon as possible (i.e. 'swift trust') instead of focusing on social exchanges.*
The highest frequency is at 6.0 (moderate) and at 10.0 (high agreement). There is a bi-modality.

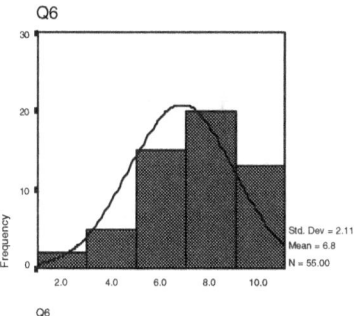

Q6: *In a virtual team, I usually believe that my team partners are competent.*
The frequencies are right skewed whilst the highest frequency is at 8.0.

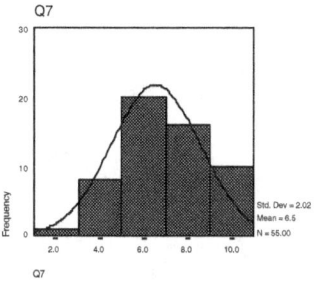

Q7: *In a virtual team, I usually believe that my team partners have a good level of 'interpersonal skills'.*
The frequencies are almost normally distributed around 6.0.

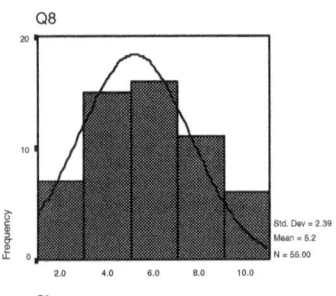

Q8: *In a virtual team, I believe my team partners think and act like I do when it comes to concrete things.* The frequencies are left skewed and the highest frequency is at 6.0.

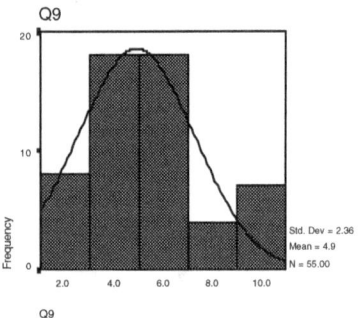

Q9: *In a virtual team, I find it easy to predict the action of my 'virtual' colleagues.* The highest frequency is at 6.0 (moderate) and at 4.0 (above moderate). There is a bi-modality.

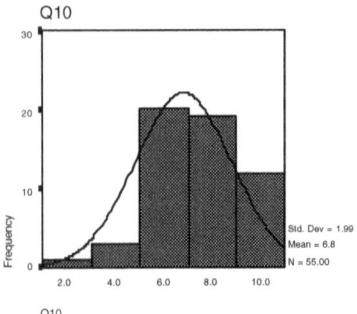

Q10: *In a virtual team, I believe my team partners display good will when interacting with each other.* The frequencies are almost normally distributed around 6.0.

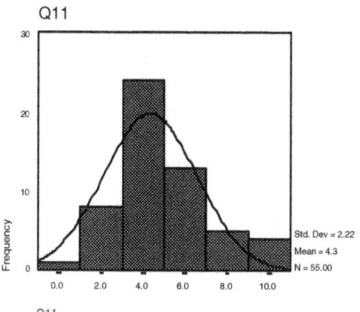

Q11: *In a virtual team, I can easily absorb some occasional acts of mistrust by others.*
The highest frequency is at level 4.0.

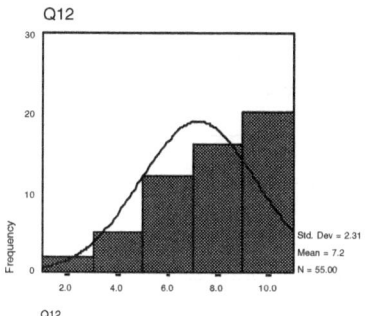

Q12: *In a virtual team, when relationships are strong and reliable, I believe trust may transfer from one person to another (through reputation effect).*
The highest frequency is at level 10.0.

5.2   Supported propositions

5.2.1   Correlation metrics

From the research made for the theory chapter (III), we assumed that the trust variables in a virtual team are independent of each other. The logical conclusion from this assumption is that there is no association (correlation) between each pair. To test this independence of the variables, we performed Pearson's correlation analysis on the opinions given by the respondents of the survey. The results of this analysis are tabulated below. The core questions 3-12 were examined for their mutual correlation within each pair. The result was obtained in the form of a matrix. Each element of the matrix included (a) the bi-variable correlation coefficient within a pair of the selected questions, and (b) the two-tailed significance level.

Specific pair	Correlation coefficient	Significance level	Inference: degree of association
Q5 against Q10	.409	.002	High
Q5 against Q12	.362	.007	High
Q6 against Q7	.641	.000	Very high
Q6 against Q8	.459	.000	Very high
Q6 against Q9	.356	.008	High
Q6 against Q10	.409	.002	High
Q6 against Q12	.362	.007	High
Q7 against Q8	.470	.000	Very high
Q7 against Q9	.405	.002	High
Q7 against Q10	.517	.000	Very high
Q8 against Q9	.374	.005	High
Q10 against Q12	.396	.003	High

Table 3: Degree of association of the variables of trust.

From the matrix (Please refer to the appendix for full details), we have found a high degree of positive parametric correlation between 12 pairs of variables. The propositions are considered to be supported if a very high—or a high—degree of correlation emerged. By a very high correlation, we mean a coefficient greater than 459 and an asymptotic significance level equal to .000. Should the correlation only be a high, it signifies the following: 356 > coef. > 459 . Meanwhile, the asymptotic significance level is inferior or equal to .007.

Further examination of these highly correlated questions indicates a certain level of positive association between them i.e. they move in the same direction: if one increases, the other one will follow suit. For instance: Q6 against Q7 (coef. =.641) have a definite interrelationship since Q6 endeavours to expose the opinion of "competence of colleagues" and Q7 attempts to picture the opinion of a "belief in the interpersonal skills of colleagues". Therefore the intensity of the opinions expressed by the respondents on Q6 is likely to re-enforce the intensity of their opinions expressed on Q7. Hence, a positive correlation is expected. In the management perspective, this interprets as follows. Belief in interpersonal ability fosters the emergence of competences among staff and promotes team spirit.

In the light of this finding, we have re-drawn the trust variables in a diagrammatic form which is presented in the subsequent page.

5.2.2   Cross-tabulations

We performed a number of cross-tabulation (Please refer to the appendix) to determine statistical significance among the level of responses to various questions by the respondent's family background and by their hobby. We also undertook Chi-square test to check the significance level. If significance is inferior or equal to .01, it is highly significant which means there is a bias. If significance level is greater than .01, it is not significant. Therefore, there is no bias.

It is expected that the opinions given by the survey respondents be influenced by their level of education, of exposure to modern technology including IT. A selection of questions was included in the survey to determine these demographic data and technological experience of the respondents. In addition, a question was asked to uncover their loyalty to their employing organisation. The core questions (Q3-Q12) were cross-tabulated against the questions Q24a, Q24e, Q25 and Q32 which revealed the significance of such cross referencing. The results of a selection of cross-tabulations are given below, together with the x^2 statistic (chi-square) and significance level.

5.2.3   Link with the literature

Support
Our findings corroborated the view expressed in the existing literature (Markus, 1994) that ascertained digital exchanges over the long term, can generate a "cold and impersonal" interaction (p. 520). By the same token, as Zack (1993) posited, the psychological closeness (p. 211) of the team members rests on the wealth of the prevailing collective interpretative background. However, the interviews of the project managers confirmed that these features can be enhanced by team-building exercises.

Consistent with some part of the research of Jarvenpaa *et al* (1998), the results indicated that the frequent interaction feature as a recursive attribute of virtual teams. High degrees of interaction have a propensity to curb vagueness and uncertainty and ought to reinforce confidence in teams. Respondents also conversed regularly and offered widespread responses among them and displayed an heavy absorption in the task & work load and extensive hours

Loose links
Yet, there are also propositions that are not fully supported by the findings. This may offer us an opportunity to re-interpret the theory spelled out in the literature review (Chapter III). For instance, the concept of *Swift trust* developed by Jarvenpaa *et al* (1998) did not strongly appeared in the respondent's

behaviour. This may be due to the fact that the aforementioned study focused exclusively on a rather short duration (8 weeks) within a non-corporate setting (EMBA students), with the perspective to "never work again together". Furthermore, our research primarily focused on what Korsgaard (1995) calls 'intact teams' i.e. "a pre-existing, relatively permanent team of employees", as opposed to the temporary group studied by Jarvenpaa *et al*. However, we specifically chose to study intact teams in order to test the power of trust in the most stringent of contexts, one in which there already existed a history, values, and norms and that relationships accumulates over time.

In addition, the 3 managers interviewed agreed upon a delay of 2 to 3 months for trust to emerge. This tends to alter the opinion posited by Jarvenpaa *et al* through the concept of 'Swift Trust' that is expected to be present from the outset. (Please refer to the theory review, Chapter III). It may be due to the type of teams associated with *Swift Trust* i.e. mainly temporary ones whereas our study was focused on corporate, thus more long-term oriented teams. We found that one of the most salient vehicles for trust to come to light appears to be embedded in the mutual support and by the opportunity physically to gather and address a pending / unsolved concern thoroughly.

Rotter's conception of trust (1967) and the associated ability to handle mistrust may be confined to a face-to-face setting. Our research indicated that once trust was breached within a virtual team (by a team member *vis-à-vis* the supervisor), it seems very unlikely that the manager will take further risk with the team member. On the contrary, should the breach of trust occur among team members, the managers indicated that they would be more prone to find an internal solution.
A more recent study carried out by Sitkin and Roth (1993) appears more in line with our findings. These writers discovered that a lawful device for restoring breach of confidence frequently has the adverse consequence of producing distrust.

Figure 1: <u>**DEPENDENTS VARIABLES of TRUST in VIRTUAL TEAMS**</u>

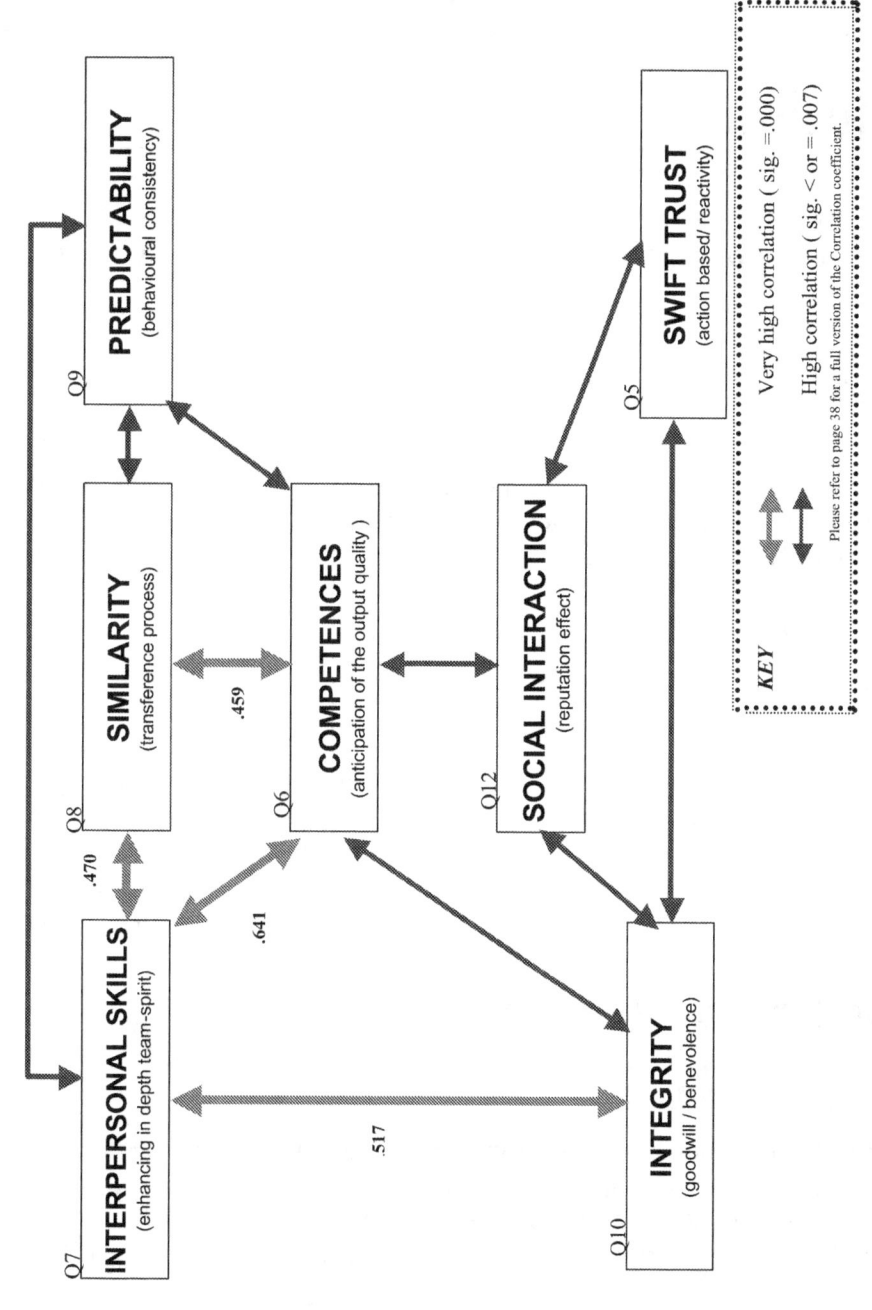

Chapter VI

Conclusion

The view of the managers based on the results of the survey

6.1   Context

As the Consultant Stephen Coates, Fellow of the IPD and former manager at Scottish & Newcastle and Thames Water, puts it, global virtual teams are quite challenging since the success of these teams impinge on a the following paradox. How to reconcile the virtual attribute—i.e. etymologically "very close"—with the global requirements—i.e. "very far"?

How to handle a virtual team efficiently?

6.2   Procedure

Two project directors and one project manager, working for a telecom company operating in 75 countries, were interviewed on the phone for 2 hours each. The three interviewed team managers were enjoying a team management experience of 10 to 15 years in a face-to-face context and at least 3 years in a virtual setting. The primary focus of the questions was the results of the survey and how to foster a trust atmosphere. Therefore, their expertise enables us to put the results of the survey into perspective.

6.3   Challenges of virtual team management

6.3.1   Different hours of work.

How to channel information downward from the manager to each employee at the same time? Whilst in conference-calls with some time lapse that extend beyond 6 hours. Some project manger indicated that concern often arise with Australia as there are no decent overlapping hours with Asia (Singapore, Honk Kong), Europe (Paris, Brussels or London) and America (Washington D.C.).

6.3.2   The distance concern: Scarcity of informality & personal information

The manager must make sure that he has a good understanding of the situation which is influenced by distance, language and media coldness (none or little body language). The richness of a conventional relationship arises from the informality that develops among team members. For instance, whilst waiting for the late arrival of others to a meeting, informal communication may manifest itself provided that attendants share a common background (e.g. widely practised sports like soccer). In most European countries like France or Italy, it has been observed that these employees will engage in conversation quite swiftly. A higher feeling of risk is re-enforced by the rare occurrence of informal relationships. In a face-to-face context, basic daily behaviour such as shaking hands, saying hello, even informal meeting in the corridor or lift enable a manager to gauge the mood of the employee they will deal within the day or week Therefore, when somebody is uncomfortable, the manager can adapt his behaviour towards the person in real time.

Furthermore, in a traditional setting, the sartorial code offers insights on the image that individuals want to establish. Their clothing style may hint at indicating their social class or their casual life style (e.g., casual Friday in the US). Conventional teams enjoy a higher closeness highlighting a less ambiguous interpretation of their reference system. Therefore, it facilitates the anticipation of future behaviour or understanding of current deeds.

In a global virtual context, first identification is focused on the name spelling—to infer alleged origins—and the tone voice. However, it is rather risky to guess the ethnic origins from the outset.
As a result, any inappropriate humour may have a devastating effect on team spirit especially considering the coldness and asynchronous attributes of the media (e.g., e-mail).

6.3.3   Turn-over & Performance reward

The relationship to the company differs according to the context. In America, employees are usually more short-term oriented as they feel themselves freer *vis-à-vis* their company. Generally speaking, they change companies more often than in continental Europe and *a fortiori* to Asia. This heightens the risk for the remote manager. Faced with these high employees turn-over rates, managers are challenged by the dissimilarities in wages among the various zone. For instance, there is a marked discrepancy between the wages increase in the US, and the European continental customs. All performances being equal, a manager asserted that pay rise in the US was on average twice as high as a country like Belgium. A fairly similar trend has been observed between the UK and the rest of Europe.

6.3.4   Cultural dissimilarities

One of the worst situations arises when a manager has identified a concern but—owing to cultural difference—is unable to determine the appropriate action to correct it. Several European managers reported their lack of analytic system to penetrate the intricacies of Asian employees. These team members usually display a great deal of reserve and it is not rare that managers must ask them their opinion three times before getting a satisfactory answer. Here, the respect of the hierarchy may be of the utmost importance. On the contrary, the same supervisors mentioned that Americans would more easily feel obliged to shed light on a particular subject clearly stating the pros and the cons.

6.3.5   The sub-teams.

When there are some sub-teams i.e. a large team is further divided into a cascade of smaller teams, the likelihood of conflicts occurring is even greater than face-to-face context. Some sub-teams want their ideas or project be recognized as the path to follow. However, the decision which was made challenged their initial goals by supporting another view. This type of situation is easier to handle in a face-to-face setting just as resentment, dealt with on a daily basis, is accommodated more swiftly.
Obviously, this may endanger trust within the virtual team.

6.4   Proposed solutions

6.4.1   Physical meeting at the outset of the project..

Working out a plan for the project including the main distribution of roles and duties, setting up of milestones and shedding light on the rules and regulations of the team may help as well. If the team member agreed upon the plan, then it will not be possible to deviate from it during the implementation of the project. Furthermore, being physically gathered as a complete entity in a single place heightens the adhesion to the project and helps participants clarifying avenues directly topic-related. Therefore, the manager can easily check the feed-back of the team on the plan and its proposed deadlines and, if necessary, adjust it to reach a strong agreement, which is a key prerequisite to a smooth running of the forthcoming virtual working relationship. This opportunity is rather impractical to achieve in a virtual setting.

6.4.2   Team-building exercise.

As discussed, in a virtual setting, the informality may be more tenuous to surface. As people need to connect at unearthly hours like 7.00 am or 8.00 pm, the late arrival of team members may occur even more frequently than in conventional settings. Therefore, there is need for humanising the relationship. Prior team-building (face-to-face) exercises may enable attendants to broach other topics than strictly professional matters. For example, hearing a baby crying, a team member may inquire about the infant or the family, thus fostering a climate of confidence. Without a team-building exercise, a common background—other than the weather conditions in the originating country—may fail to emerge. How can Europeans broach the informal topic of soccer with Americans? Or *vice versa* with baseball? Thus, the difficulty is to shift from a professional rapport to a more human relationship that strengthens teamwork.

There are no rules but organising a stress-free evening to physically gather all the team members seems to have positive effect on a group as an introductory session. A play and participating activity (such as bowling rather than theatre) appears significantly to develop a feeling of physical acquaintance among the team members which is of utmost importance for the subsequent professional remote interpersonal relations that will occur. It has been noted that this type of gathering allows individuals to get to know each other, differently from in a professional context. More specifically, people who were able to grasp some information about 'family life' (number of children, occupation of the spouse..) were then eager to recall this information (when back to their far-flung countries) in later encounters—e.g. when waiting for the other team member to join a conference-call-, thus deepening the trust-oriented relationship.

Tools (enablers)

Although the breakthroughs permit a better and more efficient communication round the globe, these tools may only be considered as 'stopgap measure' facilitated by the technology. The idea that a virtual team could be managed with as much proximity and easiness as a face-to-face team remains at best a dream or an illusion.

6.4.3   Access to a virtual data base.

The most efficient appears to be the e-mail. To carry pictures or drawing (flip-chart), the video-conference may be appropriate. But what is important here is to ensure a structure that enables sharing of document. To give access to a data-base to the virtual team members dealing with shared information i.e. a virtual place where the virtual colleagues will apprise the team of the state of progress of the others' work. This creates a favourable climate for trust to come to light. A feeling of transparency may emerge from the input of the virtual colleagues (content), the methodology and the available information on the project. This reduces the usual information retention syndrome. Associates may then have access to the minutes of the meetings (tele—or video-conference) and to the intermediate work (work in progress).

6.4.4   Detailed reports

The virtual setting heightens the need for more formalised reports than in a face-to-face context. Remote teams require more emphasis on the tasks details, as the attendance of the all the team members is subject to time zone availability (*ad hoc* hours). Obviously, the way to express oneself varies to a great extent between oral and writing communication. Writing requires more time and more detail, thus increasing the formal tone. In a conventional setting, the minutes of meetings about projects are usually more succinct as the tasks are not fully developed in fine detail. The status of progress of the tasks may be summarized by a sentence like 'all is proceeding according to plans'. Moreover, these detailed reports should help to reduce the common human bias for developing a piece of a project on one's own and revealing at the last moment when it is 'polished'. Indeed, the team member keeps silent on the topic with a view to 'offer' it to one's manager and anticipates that he will be applauded.

One of the most difficult situations is when a manager sheds light on the way to achieve a task. For instance, although the associate already committed him/herself heavily to a topic, the supervisor has to clarify the appropriate procedure to deal with the assignment, usually by making it simpler. Then, the colleague may look desperate and feel 'I worked for nothing'.

6.4.5 Need for increased control

As the delegation process is more significant, several managers insisted on the heightened need for control. The agreement to clear and specific milestones together with frequent appraisals—one every six months on average—are recommended. However, these appraisals should not give rise to any surprising results. When issues arise, managers ought to get their message through informally—waiting for the assessment may be too late—, whereas when good news surfaces, supervisors should spread it enthusiastically as soon as possible.

Furthermore, a team leader's business trips are also encouraged to apprehend physically the business unit and the atmosphere on site. A visit paid to each business venue once per month seems to be the trend. Whilst these visits aim at solving concerns such as 'handling of free-riders' (Please refer to the theory chapter, Chapter III), the ultimate goal of these trips is to reassure the local team members and to inspire trust within the team.

Here, the role of senior supervisor that can display expertise and respect is crucial to prevent any possible breach of trust such as lack of honesty—untrue information on the level of progress of a task— or mediocrity—inaccurate information on the team member's own abilities.

6.4.6 What can be established:

- Detailed activity report
- Catalogue of difficulties encountered
- Check overlapping of assignments (to avoid an acrimonious selecting decision that may endanger team spirit and eventually the efficiency of the team)

6.5 Ideal size of a team and Characteristics of virtual team member

6.5.1 Ideal size

Due to technical constraints, the maximum size appears to be between 6 and 8 members. Above 8 colleagues, tele-conference may shift into inaudible conversations. Therefore, the creation of sub-teams may alleviate this concern with representatives that will channel the information down to the other employees. Although the results of the survey evaluated the ideal average total duration of a virtual team at 8 months, many managers we interviewed insisted on a time lapse between 1 and 3 years (within a project structure). In addition, one mentioned that there was not necessarily any time boundaries.

6.5.2 Characteristics of the ideal virtual team member

Sine-qua non conditions:
To be able to exchange information at the appropriate time.
To know how to request the suitable assistance and support of both manager and others team members.
Understanding of how one's work comes within the scope of the overall process:
To be able to carry the information down the hierarchy

To be cognizant of the fact that the piece that the associate is responsible for is included in an overall process. Therefore, it not necessary to attempt to achieve a state of the art work if it generates further delay and inconsistency with the whole body of the assignment. The team member must think and act as one completely dependent on the others.

6.5.3   How to face the cultural differences?

Faced with the enthusiasm of the Americans or the extreme politeness of the Asian, the European manager should not attempt to embark on mimicry. Whilst in a bi-national relationship, it may not always ring true but within tri-nationals, there are good grounds for saying that the consistency may be prone to be impossible especially in simultaneous conference-calls. The interviewed managers stressed the fact that playing in their field may primarily increase the tier of risk without solving the issue. Actually, it may appear as a presumption on what the employees are expecting where it is rationally not feasible to be American and Asian at the same time without generating misunderstandings. What is of core significance here is to shed light on the 'translation tables' to the team members i.e. how the manager operates. For instance, when I say "I am happy", it should be interpreted or read as "I am very happy" by an American. By the same token, if the manager asserts "It could be better", it clearly signifies "Start all over again"! As a result, the most efficient fashion over the long term could be encapsulated as follows: stay yourself, with clear initial emphasis on the interpreting rules.

Moreover, tackling of questions that may seem mundane in a face-to-face setting is highly desirable in a virtual relationship. Clarifying avenues such as: 'What do you expect from me' and 'what do I expect from you' are crucial since the manager does not see the feedback on their faces.

6.6   Media appropriateness

Among the team managers, a consensus seemed to emerge about common rules for the employment of the following media:

6.6.1   Conference-calls:

For progress reports: once a week
For a specific topic: twice to three times a month

6.6.2   E-mail:

Definition of topics to be carbon copied on.

6.6.3   Video-conference

Useful for flip-chart (drawing): no language barriers
Issues: expensive and inflexible as it requires a formerly-agreed allocated slot hours 50% of the participants usually feel unease at seeing themselves on the screen or looking at the camera.

6.6.4   Telephone:

For immediate response

REFERENCES

1. Argyris, C. 1960. Understanding organizational behaviour. Homewood, IL:Dorsey.

2. Arrow 1974, The limits of Organizations. New York: Norton.

3. Axelrod, R. 1984. The evolution of cooperation. New York: Basic Books.

4. Barber, B. 1983. The logic and limits of trust. New Brunswick, NJ: Rutgers University Press.

5. Barnard, C. 1938. The functions of the executive. Cambridge, MA: Harvard University Press.

6. Barney, J. B., & Hansen, M. H. 1994. Trustworthiness as a source of competitive advantage. Strategic Management Journal 15: 175-190.

7. Baldwin, M. W. 1992. Relational schemas and the processing of social information Psychological Bulletin, 112: 461484.

8. Beardwell & Holden . 1999. International Human Management. London, Pitman Publishing.

9. Besanko, D., Dranove D., Shanley M. 1998. Economics of strategy. 2nd edition. New York: Wiley.

10. Blau, P. M. 1964. Exchange and power in social life. New York: Wiley.

11. Bradach, J., & Eccles, R. 1989. Price, authority, and trust: From ideal types to plural forms. Annual Review of Sociology, 15: 97-118.

12. Brewer, M. B., & Silver, M. 1978. Ingroup bias as a function of task characteristics. European Journal of Social Psychology, 8: 393-400.

13. Bromiley, P., St Cummings, L. L. 1995. Transaction costs in organizations with trust. In R. Bies, B. Sheppard, & R. Lewicki (Eds.), Research on negotiations in organizations, vol. 5: 219-247. Greenwich, CT: JAI Press.

14. Browning, L.D., Beyer, J.M. & Shetler, J.C. 1995; Building cooperation in a competitive industry: Sematech and the semiconductor industry. Academy of Management Journal, 38: 113-151.

15. Butler, J. K., Jr. 1991. Towards understanding and measuring conditions of trust: Evolution of a conditions of trust inventory. Journal of Management, 17: 643-663.

16. Child J. 1998. Trust and International Strategic Alliances: The Case of Sino-Foreign Joint Ventures. In Lane & Bachman, 1998, "Trust within and between organisations", New York: Oxford University Press.

17. Chiles, T. H., & McMacklin, J. F. 1996. Integrating variable risk preferences, trust, and transaction cost economics. Academy of Management Review, 21: 73-99.

18. Coleman, J. S. 1990. Foundations of social theory. Cambridge, MA: Belknap Press of Harvard University.

19. Cook, J., & Wall, T. 1980. New work attitude measures of trust, organizational commitment, and personal need nonfulfillment. Journal of Occupational Psychology. 53: 39-52.

20. Cox, T., Jr., & Tung, R. L. 1997. The multicultural organization revisited. In C. L. Cooper & S. E. Jackson (Eds.), Creating tomorrow's organizations: A handbook for future research in organizational behaviour. 7-28. London:Wiley.

21. Creed, W. E. D., & Miles, R. E. 1996. Trust in organizations: A conceptual framework linking organizational forms, managerial philosophies, and the opportunity costs of controls. In R. M. Kramer & T.

R. Tyler (Eds.), Trust in organizations: Frontiers of theory and research: 16-38. Thousand Oaks, CA: Sage.

22. Cummings, L.L., and Bromiley, P. The organizational trust inventory (OTI): development and validation. In R.M. Kramer and T.R. Tyler (eds.), Trust in Organizations: Frontiers of Theory and Research. Thousand Oaks, CA: Sage Publications, 1996, pp. 302-330.

23. Darley, J. M., St Berscheid, E. 1967. Increased liking as a result of anticipation of personal contact. Human Relations, 20: 29-40.

24. Dasgupta, P. 1988. Trust as a commodity. In D. Gambetta (Ed.), Trust: Making and breaking cooperative relations: 49-72. Cambridge, MA: Basil Blackwell.

25. D'Aveni, R. A. 1994. Hypercompetition: Managing the dynamics of strategic maneuvering. New York: Free Press. Dawes, R. M., & Thaler, R. H. 1988. Cooperation. Journal of Economic Perspectives, 2: 187-197.

26. Davis, F. D., & Kotteman, J. E. 1994. User perceptions of decision support effectiveness: Two production planning experiments. Decision Sciences, 25: 57-77.

27. Deutsch, M. Trust and suspicion. Journal of Conflict Resolution, 2 (1958), 265-279.

28. Deutsch, M. 1960. The effect of motivational orientation upon trust and suspicion. Human Relations, 13: 123-139.

29. Deutsch, M. 1962. Cooperation and trust: Some theoretical notes. In M. R. Jones (Ed.), Nebraska Symposium on Motivation: 275-317. Lincoln: University of Nebraska Press.

30. Deutsch, M., & Krauss, R. M. 1960. The effect of threat upon interpersonal bargaining. Journal of Abnormal and Social Psychology, 61: 181-189.

31. Dickens, Peter; (1997) The global shift, transforming the world economy, London: Chapman & Hall, Third edition.

32. Dion, K. K., Berscheid, E., & Walster, E. 1972. What is beautiful is good. Journal of Personality and Social Psychology, 24: 285-290.

33. Doney P.M., Cannon J.P., Mullen M.R.; July 1998; Understanding the influence of national culture on the development of trust. Academy of Management. The Academy of Management Review; Mississippi State.

34. Dore, R. 1983; Goodwill and the spirit of market capitalism. British Journal of Sociology, 34: 459-482.

35. Eisenhardt, K.M. Building theories from case study research. Academy of Management Review, 14, 4 (1989), 532-550.

36. Eisenhardt, K. M., & Tabrizi, B. N. 1995. Accelerating adaptive processes: Product innovation in the global computer industry. Administrative Science Quarterly, 40: 84-110.

37. Ekeh, P. P. 1974. Social exchange theory: The two traditions. Cambridge, MA: Harvard University Press.

38. Erikson, E. H. 1963. Childhood and society (2nd ed.). New York: Norton.

39. Fama, E. F., & Jensen, M. C. 1983. Agency problems and residual claims. Journal of Law and Economics, 26: 301325.

40. Farnsworth, E. A. 1982. Contracts. Boston: Little, Brown.

41. Farris, G.F.; Senner, E.E.; and Butterfield, D.A. Trust, culture, and organizational behavior. Industrial Relations, 12 (1973), 144-157.

42. Fichman, M. 1997. A multilevel analysis of trust in interorganizational customer-supplier ties. Paper presented at the annual meeting of the Academy of Management, Boston.

43. Fiske, A. P. 1990. Relativity within Moose culture: Four incommensurable models for social relationships. Ethos, 18: 180-204.

44. Fiske, S. T., & Taylor, S. E. 1984. Social cognition. Reading, MA: Addison-Wesley.

45. Folger, R., & Konovsky, M. A. 1989. Effects of procedural and distributive justice on reactions to pay raise decisions. Academy of Management Journal, 32: 115-130.

46. Fukuyama, F. 1995. Trust: The social virtues and the creation of prosperity. New York: Free Press.

47. Furst, S.; Blackburn, R. & Rosen, B., Virtual team effectiveness: a proposed research agenda, 249.

48. Gabarro, J. J. 1978. The development of trust influence and expectations. In A. G. Athos & J. J. Gabarro (Eds.), Interpersonal behavior: Communication and understanding in relationships: 290-303. Englewood Cliffs, NJ: PrenticeHall.

49. Gambetta, D. 1988. Can we trust trust? In D. Gambetta (Ed.), Trust: Making and breaking cooperative relations: 213237. Cambridge, MA: Basil Blackwell.

50. Ganesan, S. 1994; Determinants of long-term orientation in buyer-seller relationships. Journal of marketing, 58 (2): &-19.

51. Giddens A. 1994. The Constitution of Society. Cambridge: Polity Press.

52. Giffin, K. 1967. The contribution of studies of source credibility to a theory of interpersonal trust in the communication process. Psychological Bulletin, 68: 104-120.

53. Gomez-Mejia, L. R., & Balkin, D. B. 1992. Determinants of faculty pay: An agency theory perspective. Academy of Management Journal 35: 921-955.

54. Govier, T. 1994. Is it a jungle out there? Trust, distrust and the construction of social reality. Dialogue, XXXII: 237-252.

55. Graen, G. B., & Uhl-Bien, M. 1995. Relationship-based approach to leadership: Development of leader-member exchange (LMX) theory of leadership over 25 years: Applying a multi-level multi-domain perspective. Leadership Quarterly, 6: 219-247.

56. Granovetter, M. 1985. Economic action and social structure: The problem of embeddedness. American Journal of Sociology, 91: 481-510.

57. Gulatti, R. 1995. Does familiarity breed trust? The implications of repeated ties for contractual choice in alliances. Academy of Management Journal 38: 85-112.

58. Hamel, G., & Prahalad, C. K.1994. Competing for the future. Boston: Harvard Business School Press.

59. Hammer, M., & Champy, J. 1993. Re-engineering the corporation: A manifesto for business revolution. New York: HarperBusiness.

60. Hardin, R. 1993. The street-level epistemology of trust. Politics & Society, 21: 505-529.

61. Harrison, P. D., & Harrell, A. 1993. Impact of 'adverse selection' on managers' project evaluation decisions. Academy of Management Journal, 36: 635-643.

62. Hart, K. M., Capps, H. R., Cangemi, J. P., & Caillouet, L. M. 1986. Exploring organizational trust and its multiple dimensions: A case study of General Motors. Organization Development JournaL 4(2): 3139.

63. Hill, C. W., & Jones, T. M. 1992. Stakeholder-agency theory. Journal of Management Studies, 29: 131-154.

64. Hofstede, G. 1991. Cultures and organisations: software of the Mind. London: Mac Graw Hill.

65. Holmes, J. G. 1991. Trust and the appraisal process in close relationships. In W. H. Jones & D. Perlman (Eds.), Advances in personal relationships, vol. 2: 57-104. London: Jessica Kingsley.

66. Hosmer, L. T. 1995. Trust: The connecting link between organizational theory and philosophical ethics. Academy of Management Review, 20: 379-403.

67. Jarvenpaa S.L.; Knoll, K. and Leidner D. (Spring 1998) Is anybody out there? Antecedents of trust in global virtual teams. Journal of Management Information Systems; Armonk.

68. Jennings, E. E. 1971. Routes to the executive suite. New York: McGraw-Hill.

69. Jensen, M. C., & Meckling, W. C. 1976. Theory of the firm: Managerial behavior, agency costs, and ownership structure. Journal of Financial Economics, 3: 305-360.

70. Johnson-George, C., & Swap, W. C. 1982. The measurement of specific interpersonal trust: Construction and validation of a scale to assess trust in a specific other. Journal of Personality and Social Psychology, 34: 1306-1317.

71. Kee, H. W., & Knox, R. E. 1970. Conceptual and methodological considerations in the study of trust. Journal of Conflict Resolution, 14: 357-366.

72. Konovsky, M. A., & Cropanzano, R. 1991. Perceived fairness of employee drug testing as a predictor of employee attitudes and job performance. Journal of Applied Psychology, 78: 698-707.

73. Kramer, R. M., & Brewer, M. B. 1984. Effects of group identity on resource use in a simulated commons dilemma. Journal of Personality and Social Psychology, 46: 1944-1957.

74. Kramer, R. M., & Brewer, M. B. 1986. Social group identity and the emergence of cooperation in resource conversation dilemmas. Frankfurt, Germany: Peter Lang Publishing.

75. Kramer, R.M.; Brewer, M.B.; and Hanna, B.A. Collective trust and collective action: the decision to trust as a social decision. In R.M. Kramer and T.R. Tyler (eds.), Trust in Organizations: Frontiers of Theory and Research. Thousand Oaks, CA: Sage Publications,1996, pp. 357-389.

76. Kramer and Tyler .1996. Trust in Organisations, Frontiers of Theory and Research. Thousands Oaks/CA: Sage Publications.

77. Lane & Bachman, 1998, "Trust within and between organisations", New York: Oxford University Press.

78. Langer, E. J. 1975. The illusion of control. Journal of Personality and Social Psychology, 32: 311-328.

79. Larzelere, R.E., and Huston, T.L. The dyadic trust scale: toward understanding trust in close relationships. Journal of Marriage and the Family (August 1980), 595604.

80. Laurent, A. 1983. The cultural diversity of Western conceptions of Management. In 'International Studies of Management and organisation, Vol. 13, Nos 1-2, Spring-Summer.

81. Lawler, E. 1992. The ultimate advantage: Creating the high involvement organization. San Francisco: Jossey-Bass.

82. Lewicki, R. J., & S Bunker, B. B. 1995a. Developing and maintaining trust in work relationships. In R. M. Kramer & T. R. Tyler (Eds.), Trust in organizations: Frontiers of theory and research: 114-139. Thousand Oaks, CA: Sage.

83. Lewicki, R. J., & Bunker, B. B. 1995b. Trust in relationships: A model of development and decline. In B. B. Bunker, J. Z. Rubin, & Associates (Eds.), Conflict, cooperation, and justice: 133-173. San Francisco: Jossey-Bass.

84. Lipnack, J., and Stamps, J. Virtual Teams: Reaching across Space, Time, and Organizations with Technology. New York: John Wiley, 1997.

85. Luce, R. D., & Raiffa, H. 1957. Games and decisions: Introduction and critical survey. New York: Wiley.

86. Luhmann, N. 1979. Trust and power. New York: Wiley.

87. Markus, M.L. Electronic mail as the medium of managerial choice. Organization Science, 5, 4 (November 1994), 502-527.

88. Mayer, R.C.; Davis, J.H.; and Schoorman, F.D. An integrative model of organizational trust. Academy of Management Review, 20, 3 (1995), 709-734.

89. Mellinger, G. D. 1956. Interpersonal trust as a factor in communication. Journal of Abnormal and Social Psychology 52: 304-309.

90. Meyerson, D.; Weick, K.E.; and Kramer, R.M. Swift trust and temporary groups. In R.M. Kramer and T.R. Tyler (eds.), Trust in Organizations: Frontiers of Theory and Research. Thousand Oaks, CA: Sage Publications, 1996, pp. 166195.

91. Miles, R.E., and Snow, C.C. Causes of failures in network organizations. California Management Review (Summer 1992), 53-72.

92. Mishra, A. K. 1996. Organizational responses to crisis: The centrality of trust. In R. M. Kramer & T. R. Tyler (Eds.), Trust in organizations: Frontiers of theory and research: 261-287. Thousand Oaks, CA: Sage.

93. Moorman, C., Zaltman, G., & Deshpande, R. 1992. Relationships between providers and users of market research: The dynamics of trust within and between organizations. Journal of Marketing Research, 29: 314-328.

94. Muchinsky, P. M. 1977. An intraorganizational analysis of the Roberts and O'Reilly organizational communication questionnaire. Journal of Applied Psychology, 62: 184188.

95. Murnighan, J. K. 1991. The dynamics of bargaining games. Englewood Cliffs, NJ: Prentice-Hall.

96. McAllister, D.J. Affect—and cognition-based trust as foundations for interpersonal cooperation in organizations. Academy of Management Journal, 38, 1 (1995), 24-59.

97. McKnight D. Harrison, Cummings Larry L, Chervany Norman L . Jul 1998. Initial trust formation in new organizational relationships, Academy of Management. The Academy of Management Review. Mississippi State. Volume: 23, Issue: 3, Pagination: 473-490. ISSN: 03637425.

98. North, D. C. 1990. Institutions, institutional change, and economic performance. New York: Cambridge University Press.

99. Nooteboom, B. 1996. Trust, opportunism, and governance: A process and control model. Organization Studies, 17: 985-1010.

100. Nooteboom, B., Berger, H., Hz Noorderhaven, N. G. 1997. Effects of trust and governance on relational risk. Academy of Management Journal, 40: 308-338.

101. Noordevier, T.G., John, G. & Nevin, J.R. ; 1990; Performance outcomes of purchasing arrangements in industrial buyer-vendor relationships. Journl of Marketing, 54 (4): 80-93.

102. Orbell, J., Dawes, R., & Schwartz-Shea, P. 1994. Trust, social categories, and individuals: The case of gender. Motivation and Emotion, 18: 109-128.

103. O'Reilly, C. A., III. 1977. Supervisors and peers as information sources, group supportiveness, and individual decision-making performance. Journal of Applied Psychology, 62: 632-635.

104. O'Reilly, C. A., III, & Roberts, K. H. 1974. Information filtration in organizations: Three experiments. Organizational Behavior and Human Performance, ll: 253-265.

105. O'Reilly, C. A., III, & Roberts, K. H. 1977. Task group structure, communication, and effectiveness in three organizations. Journal of Applied Psychology, 62: 674-681.

106. Paese, P. W., & Sniezek, J. A. 1991..Influences on the appropriateness of confidence in judgment: Practice, effort, information, and decision-making. Organizational Behavior and Human Decision Processes, 48: 100-130.

107. Pearce, J. L., Bigley, G. A., & Branyiczki, I. In press. Procedural justice as modernism: Placing industrial/organizational psychology in context. Applied Psychology: An International Review.

108. Powell, W. W. 1996. Trust-based forms of governance. In R. M. Kramer & T. R. Tyler (Eds.), Trust in organizations: Frontiers of theory and research: 51-67. Thousand Oaks, CA: Sage.

109. Read, W. H. 1962. Upward communication in industrial hierarchies. Human Relations, 15(3): 3-15.

110. Rempel, J. K., Holmes, J. G., & Zanna, M. P. 1985. Trust in close relationships. Journal of Personality and Social Psychology, 49: 95-112.

111. Riker, W. H. 1971. The nature of trust. In J. T. Tedeschi (Ed.), Perspectives on social power: 63-81. Chicago: Aldine.

112. Ring, P. S. 1996. Fragile and resilient trust and their roles in economic exchange. Business & Society, 35: 148-175.

113. Ring, P. S., & Van de Ven, A. H. 1989. Formal and informal dimensions of transactions. In A. H. Van de Ven, H. Angle, & M. S. Poole (Eds.), Research on the management of innovation: The Minnesota studies: 171-192. New York: Ballinger.

114. Ring, P. S., & Van de Ven, A. 1992. Structuring cooperative relations between organizations. Strategic Management Journal 13: 483-498.

115. Roberts, K. H., & O'Reilly, C. A., III. 1974a. Failures in upward communication in organizations: Three possible culprits. Academy of Management Journal 17: 205-215.

116. Roberts, K. H., & O'Reilly, C. A., III. 1974b. Measuring organizational communication. Journal of Applied Psychology, 59: 321-326.

117. Roberts, K. H., & O'Reilly, C. A., III. 1979. Some correlates of communication roles in organizations. Academy of Management Journal, 22: 42-57.

118. Robinson, S. L., & Rousseau, D. M. 1994. Violating the psychological contract: Not the exception but the norm. Journal of Organizational Behavior, 15: 245-259.

119. Rotter, J. B. 1967. A new scale for the measurement of interpersonal trust. Journal of Personality, 35: 651-665.

120. Rotter, J. B. 1971. Generalized expectancies for interpersonal trust. American Psychologist, 26: 443-452.

121. Rotter, J. B. 1980. Interpersonal trust, trustworthiness, and gullibility. American Psychologist, 35: 1-7.

122. Rousseau, D. M. 1989. Psychological and implied contracts in organizations. Employee Rights and Responsibilities Journal, 2: 121-139.

123. Rousseau, D. M. 1995. Psychological contracts in organizations: Understanding written and unwritten agreements. London: Sage.

124. Rousseau, D. M., & Parks, J. M. 1993. The contracts of individuals and organizations. In B. M. Staw & L. L. Cummings (Eds.), Research in organizational behavior, vol. 15:1-43. Greenwich, CT: JAI Press.

125. Sabel, C. F. 1993. Studied trust: Building new forms of cooperation in a volatile economy. Human Relations, 46: 1133-1170.

126. Sako M. 1992. Prices, Quality and Trust: Inter-firm Relation in Britain and Japan. Cambridge: Cambridge University Press.

127. Sapienza, H. J., & Korsgaard, M. A. 1996. Managing investor relations: The impact of procedural justice in establishing and sustaining investor support. Academy of Management Journal 39: 544-574.

128. Saunders, Lewis and Thornhill. 2000. Research methods for Business Students; 2nd Edition; Financial Times / Prentice Hall.

129. Schneider, B., & Bowen, D. E. 1995. Winning the service game. Boston: Harvard Business School Press.

130. Shaver, P. R., & Hazan, C. 1994. Attachment. In A. L. Weber & J. H. Harvey (Eds.), Perspectives on close relationships: 110-130. Boston: Allyn and Bacon.

131. Sheppard Blair H. & Sherman Dana M. Jul 1998. The grammers of trust: A model and general implications Academy of Management. The Academy of Management Review—Mississippi State. Volume: 23, Issue: 3, Pagination: 422-437, ISSN: 03637425.

132. Simmel. 1964. The sociology of George Simmel. Translation by Kurt H. Wolff (Ed.). New York: Free Press.

133. Sitkin, S. B., & Stickel, D. 1996. The road to hell: The dynamics of distrust in an era of quality. In R. M. Kramer & T. R. Tyler (Eds.), Trust in organizations: Frontiers of theory and research: 196-215. Thousand Oaks, CA: Sage.

134. Sitkin, S.B., and Roth, N.L. Explaining the limited effectiveness of legalistic "remedies" for trust/distrust. Organization Science, 4, 3 (August 1993), 367-392.

135. Taylor, S. E., & Brown, J. D. 1988. Illusion and well-being: A social psychological perspective on mental health. Psychological Bulletin, 103: 193-210.

136. Tyler, T. R. 1990. Why people obey the law. New Haven, CT: Yale University Press.

137. Walther, J.B. Group and interpersonal effects in international computer-mediated collaboration. Human Communication Research, 23, 3 (March 1997), 342-369.

138. Wanous, J. 1977. Organizational entry: Newcomers moving from outside to inside. Psychological Bulletin, 84: 601-618.

139. Wanous, J. P., Poland, T. D., Premack, S. L., & Davis, K. S. 1992. The effects of met expectations on newcomer attitudes and behaviors: A review and meta-analysis. Journal of Applied Psychology, 77: 288-297.

140. Warkentin M. & Beranek P.M., 1999 Training to improve virtual team communication. Info Systems Journal, 9, 271-289.

141. Watson-Fritz M.B., Narasimhan, S.& Rhee, H. (1998). Communication & coordination in the virtual office. Journal of Management Information Systems, 14, 7-28.

142. Whitener Ellen M., Brodt Susan E., Korsgaard M. Audrey, Werner Jon M. Jul 1998. Managers as initiators of trust: An exchange relationship framework for understanding managerial trustworthy behavior

Academy of Management. The Academy of Management Review Mississippi State. Volume: 23, Issue: 3, Pagination: 513-530, ISSN: 03637425.

143. Williamson, O. E. 1975. Markets and hierarchies. New York: Free Press.

144. Williamson, O. E. 1981. The economics of organization: The transaction cost approach. American Journal of Sociology, 87: 548-577.

145. Williamson, O. E. 1985. The economic institutions of capitalism. New York: Free Press.

146. Williamson, O. E. 1993. Calculativeness, trust, and economic organization. Journal of Law and Economics, 34: 453-502.

147. Worchel, P. 1979. Trust and distrust. In W. G. Austin 8r S. Worchel (Eds.), The social psychology of intergroup relations: 174-187. Monterey, CA: Brooks/Cole Publishing.

148. Yeager, S.J. Measurement of independent variables which affect communication: a replication of Roberts and O'Reilly. Psychological Reports (1978), 1320-1324.

149. Zack, M.H. Interactivity and communication mode choice in ongoing management groups. Information Systems Research, 4, 3 (1993), 207-238.

150. Zaheer, A., 8z Venkatraman, N. 1995. Relational governance as an interorganizational strategy: An empirical test of the role of trust in economic exchange.Strategic Management Journal, 16: 373-392.

151. Zand, D. E. 1972. Trust and managerial problem solving. Administrative Science Quarterly, 17: 229-239.

152. Zucker, L. G. 1986. Production of trust: Institutional sources of economic structure, 1840-1920. In B.M. Staw & L. L. Cummings, Research in organizational behavior, vol. 8:53-111. Greenwich, CT: JAI Press.

153. Zucker, L. G., Darby, M. R., Brewer, M. B., & Peng, Y. 1996. Collaboration structure and information dilemmas in biotechnology: Organizational boundaries and trust production. In R. M. Kramer & T. R. Tyler (Eds.), Trust in organizations: Frontiers of theory and research: 90-113. Thousand Oaks, CA: Sage.

"To be a good virtual team member, you first need to be an excellent face-to-face team partner".

A senior executive of a Fortune 500 company (London 25.08.00).

Appendix 1

The questionnaire

Please type-in your answers and send by E-MAIL the completed questionnaire by **31th August, 2000** to: anonymous@mail.rhbnc.ac.uk

Please complete all questions applicable to you. Input your answers in the grey-shaded boxes only. If you have additional comments, please add these at the end.

1. Over the last decade, has your trust in the following institutions increased, declined or levelled-off (in your home country)?
If you are a resident abroad for more than 3 years, please rank the institutions of your current host country and tick here O

a) State   trend.➤
b) Legal system
c) Police
d) Work
e) Education
f) Family
g) Religion
h) Culture
i) Sport
j) Does not apply
k) Other (please write in)

%   +   1
-   2
=   3
-
+
=
+
+
-

2. Among the following institutions, please rank the 3 insitutions which you trust the most?

1 a) State
2 b) Legal system
3 c) Police
4 d) Work
5 e) Education
6 f) Family
7 g) Religion
8 h) Culture
9 i) Sport
j) Other (please write in)

Please rank in order; top 3 only

1   2   3
➡
eg   c   e   h

You will now have 10 statements about YOUR perception of trust in a virtual team. Please, enter the appropriate number (in the grey shaded box), where 1 means you disagree very strongly and 10 you agree very strongly.

3. In a virtual team, the perception of my colleagues' trustworthiness/confidence is influenced by 'institutionals factors'
- A virtual team is defined as a group in which members physically remain on different countries, interact primarily through the use of
e-mail, telephone, call/conferences or even videoconferencing, and rarely see each other in person.
- 'Institutional factors' are elements such as if the colleague has children, if the colleague is practising his/her religion, if the colleague
holds a Certificate of a Board (e.g. CPA, lawyer...), if the colleague holds an university degree, if the colleague used to work in a well-known
corporation, if the colleague is an army reservist, if the colleague has a high level of general knowledge (culture), if the colleague is good at sports...

Please enter the appropriate number (in the grey shaded box), where 1 means you disagree very strongly and 10 you agree very strongly.

1   2   3   4   5   6   9   10   eg   5   ⬇

4. In a virtual team, in order to achieve my working goals, I depend very much on other colleagues
i.e. I depend on the avaibility of my colleagues (amount of work, family constraints..), their presence (not on leave), their mistakes, late/delay,
malevolence (breach of trust, lie, commitment not kept), bragging, release of inaccurate information, the lack of body language (versus face-to-face
as you cannot see the person, due to boundaries of the e-mail & telephone).

Please enter the appropriate number (in the grey shaded box), where 1 means you disagree very strongly and 10 you agree very strongly.

⬇

| 1 | 2 | 3 | 4 | 5 | 6 | 9 | 10 | eg | 5 | |

5. In a virtual team, I usually concentrate on action as soon as possible (i.e. 'swift trust') instead of focusing on social exchanges.
Swift Trust' is defined as a team's willingness to be pro-active from the early beginning (based on the assumption that trust is present from the start).

Please enter the appropriate number (in the grey shaded box), where 1 means you disagree very strongly and 10 you agree very strongly.

| 1 | 2 | 3 | 4 | 5 | 6 | 9 | 10 | eg | 5 | |

6. In a virtual team, I usually believe that my team partners are competent
i.e. that somebody can contribute to the project by bringing in skills directly related to the task such as concrete knowledge of a topic...

Please enter the appropriate number (in the grey shaded box), where 1 means you disagree very strongly and 10 you agree very strongly.

| 1 | 2 | 3 | 4 | 5 | 6 | 9 | 10 | eg | 5 | |

7. In a virtual team, I usually believe that my team partners have a good level of 'interpersonal skills'.
such as enthusiasm and positive tone, smooth handling of conflict, ability to listen carefully to others, proposition of optional solutions (rather than criticize when faced with a disagreement), problem solving skills, self-control, and a methodical approach (set up of milestones, acting out of clear goals, respect of time limit, explication of decision..)

Please enter the appropriate number (in the grey shaded box), where 1 means you disagree very strongly and 10 you agree very strongly.

| 1 | 2 | 3 | 4 | 5 | 6 | 9 | 10 | eg | 5 | |

8. In a virtual team, I believe my team partners think and act like I do when it comes to concrete things.
Similarity is the ability to think and act in the same direction as the other team members.

Please enter the appropriate number (in the grey shaded box), where 1 means you disagree very strongly and 10 you agree very strongly.

| 1 | 2 | 3 | 4 | 5 | 6 | 9 | 10 | eg | 5 | |

9. In a virtual team, I find it easy to predict the action of my 'virtual' colleagues
i.e. through behavioural consistency.

Please enter the appropriate number (in the grey shaded box), where 1 means you disagree very strongly and 10 you agree very strongly.

| 1 | 2 | 3 | 4 | 5 | 6 | 9 | 10 | eg | 5 | |

10. In a virtual team, I believe my team partners display good will when interacting with each other.
Good will is defined as the ability to display features like a warm welcome on the phone, a positive tone in the writing skills, a constructive attitude while in conference calls, a 'can-do' attitude, swiftness, flexibility...

Please enter the appropriate number (in the grey shaded box), where 1 means you disagree very strongly and 10 you agree very strongly.

| 1 | 2 | 3 | 4 | 5 | 6 | 9 | 10 | eg | 5 | |

11. In a virtual team, I can easily absorb some occasional acts of mistrust by others
i.e. actions that violate trust such as rule violation (violation of formal rules, changing the rules 'after the fact', breach of contract), honor violation (shirking of job responsibilities, broken promises, lying, stealing of ideas, disclosure of confidences and secrets), abusive authority, a damaged 'identity' (public criticism, accused wrongly or unfairly, insult to self or collective).

Please enter the appropriate number (in the grey shaded box), where 1 means you disagree very strongly and 10 you agree very strongly.

| 1 | 2 | 3 | 4 | 5 | 6 | 9 | 10 | eg | 5 | |

12. In a virtual team, when relationships are strong and reliable, I believe trust may transfer from one person to another (through reputation effect).

Reputation can reflect occupational aptitudes or the other trusting values: goodwill, integrity, and prospective ability. Thus, if the person has a good reputation, one will rapidly engage in trusting attitudes about that person, even without prior information.

Please enter the appropriate number (in the grey shaded box), where 1 means you disagree very strongly and 10 you agree very strongly.

| 1 | 2 | 3 | 4 | 5 | 6 | 9 | 10 | eg | 5 | |

You will now have 7 questions where you need to rank in order your 3 best propositions. Finally, you will have to identify some supplementary propositions and give your views.

13. How do you assess the goodwill of another 'virtual' colleague?

1 a) Warm welcome on the phone
2 b) Positive tone in the writing style
3 c) Enthusiasm, constructive attitude (whilst in Conference Calls)
4 d) Always willing to help
5 e) Swiftness
6 f) Flexibility
g) Other (Please write in)

Please rank in order; top 3 only

| | 1 | 2 | 3 |
| eg | c | d | f |

14. When embarking on a relationship with a NEW virtual colleague, how do you assess his/her abilities (competences)?

1 a) Diplomas / Certificates of Boards
2 b) Years of experience
3 c) Level of income (Job Title)
4 d) Quality of his/her previous work
e) Other (Please write in)

Please rank in order; top 3 only

| | 1 | 2 | 3 |
| eg | c | d | d |

15. With your 'virtual' colleagues, which repetition of the following events do you consider to endenger trust?

1 a) No answer to e-mails / phone message (within a fortnight when on duty)
2 b) Lack of availability
3 c) Release of incomplete information
4 d) Commitment not kept
5 e) Deadline not met (without prior warning notice)
6 f) Lack of observance of confidentiality
g) Other (Please write in)

Please rank in order; top 3 only

| | 1 | 2 | 3 |
| eg | c | b | d |

16. When breach of trust occurs, how do you react?

a) Do not say anything
b) Tell other people
c) Change my behaviour towards the person
d) Do not change my behaviour towards the person
e) Inform my manager (oral information)
f) Talk to the person
g) Other (Please write in)

Put a cross in the appropriate box.

1
2
3
4
5
6

17. When you identify that trust (with a 'virtual' colleague) has been damaged by yourself, how can trust be rebuilt?

Please rank in order; top 3 only

1 a) Acknowledgement of the mistake
2 b) Apologies
3 c) Straight explication
4 d) Directive from a supervisor to 'rebuild' trust
5 e) Delivering 'first class' subsequent achievement
   f) Other (Please write in)

18. In a virtual team, which of the following criteria influence your assessment of other's reputation?

Please rank in order; top 3 only

1 a) Position
2 b) Status
3 c) Age
4 d) Sex
5 e) Previous professional experiences
6 f) Quality of work
   g) Other (Please write in)

19. In a virtual team, which of the following criteria are the most detrimental to the relationship with others?

Please rank in order; top 3 only

1 a) Conflicts
2 b) Jealousy
3 c) Misunderstandings
4 d) Hurt feelings
5 e) Revenge fantasies
6 f) Pursuit of hidden agendas
   g) Other (Please write in)

20. According to your experience, what is the ideal size of a virtual team (for trust to emerge and be maintained)?

Put a cross in the appropriate box.

a) 2 members — 2
b) 3 to 5 members — 4
c) 6 to 10 members — 8
d) 11 to 15 members — 13
e) 16 to 20 members — 18
f) 21 to 30 members — 25
g) 31 to 40 members — 35
h) 41 to 49 members — 45
i) Over 50 members — 50
j) Other (Please write in)

21. According to your experience, what is the ideal duration of a virtual team (for trust to emerge and be maintained) within a project?

Please enter the appropriate number of months

22. For each of the following tasks, please select most appropriate media (i.e. telephone or conference-call, e-mail or videoconference) to sustain a trust relationship within a virtual context

	1 TEL	2 CONF- CALL	3 E-MAIL	4 VIDEO CONF.
a) To get as much information and comments as possible (on a specific subject)				
b) To avoid any misunderstanding (confirmation of what has been said on the phone or in a meeting)				
c) To complete or review of tables of data				

d) To inquire of the availibility of a person high in the hierarchy or in a
        different department (e.g. in order to set up a meeting)
e) To terminate several e-mail exchanges:to come to a conclusion and to move forward
f) To thank people for help / prompt answer
g) To transfer data / procedures
h) To make decision involving several people's output
i) To determine the allocation of the tasks, roles, responsibilities, and issue addressing
j) To request urgent information
k) To enhance building of a relationship
l) To raise, address and follow up the status of a project issue
        (through regular remote meetings)
m) To gather all the employees for a remote presentation

23. Based on YOUR experience, what are the 3 most important qualities that a 'super' virtual team member must have (for trust to emerge and be sustained)?

1   1
2   2
3   3

Many thanks for your interest hiterto and your valuable collaboration.
We are now reaching the last part of this survey (and the easiest one!)

Put a number OR a cross where applicable.

24. On average, how many of the following do you process?

Number of e-mails received (per day)
Number of e-mails sent (per day)

Number of phone-calls received (per day)
Number of phone-calls made (per day)

Number of conference-calls (per month)

25. How long have you been working for your current company?

Up to 6 months	0.6
Over 1 year to 2 years	1.5
Over 2 years to 3 years	2.5
Over 3 years to 4 years	3.5
Over 4 years to 5 years	4.5
Over 10 years	10

26. How many times did you change companies in the last 10 years?

27. How many times did you change positions (within the same company) in the last 5 years?

28. Which one of the following best describes your job?

Technical / engeneering	1	Senior Mangement	5
Supervisor	2	Directorate	6
Professional	3	Other (Please say)	
Management	4		

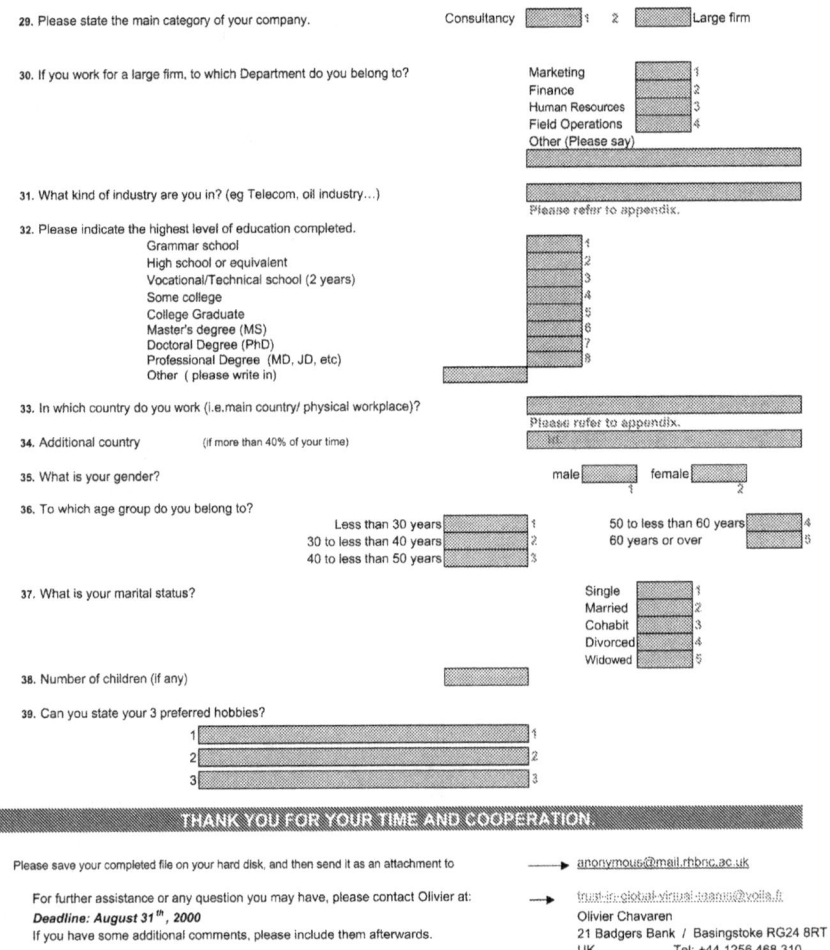

29. Please state the main category of your company.   Consultancy [_____] 1   2 [_____] Large firm

30. If you work for a large firm, to which Department do you belong to?

Marketing [_____] 1
Finance [_____] 2
Human Resources [_____] 3
Field Operations [_____] 4
Other (Please say) [_____]

31. What kind of industry are you in? (eg Telecom, oil industry…)

[_____]
Please refer to appendix.

32. Please indicate the highest level of education completed.

Grammar school [_____] 1
High school or equivalent [_____] 2
Vocational/Technical school (2 years) [_____] 3
Some college [_____] 4
College Graduate [_____] 5
Master's degree (MS) [_____] 6
Doctoral Degree (PhD) [_____] 7
Professional Degree (MD, JD, etc) [_____] 8
Other (please write in) [_____]

33. In which country do you work (i.e.main country/ physical workplace)?

[_____]
Please refer to appendix.

34. Additional country   (if more than 40% of your time)   [_____]

35. What is your gender?   male [_____] 1   female [_____] 2

36. To which age group do you belong to?

Less than 30 years [_____] 1   50 to less than 60 years [_____] 4
30 to less than 40 years [_____] 2   60 years or over [_____] 5
40 to less than 50 years [_____] 3

37. What is your marital status?

Single [_____] 1
Married [_____] 2
Cohabit [_____] 3
Divorced [_____] 4
Widowed [_____] 5

38. Number of children (if any)   [_____]

39. Can you state your 3 preferred hobbies?

1 [_____] 1
2 [_____] 2
3 [_____] 3

THANK YOU FOR YOUR TIME AND COOPERATION.

Please save your completed file on your hard disk, and then send it as an attachment to   → anonymous@mail.rhbnc.ac.uk

For further assistance or any question you may have, please contact Olivier at: → trust-in-global-virtual-teams@voila.fr
Deadline: August 31ᵗʰ, 2000   Olivier Chavaren
If you have some additional comments, please include them afterwards.   21 Badgers Bank / Basingstoke RG24 8RT
                                                                UK   Tel: +44 1256 468 310

Appendix 2

Coding Taxonomies

Appendix 2a   CODING TAXONOMY for Q23

Competences / experience 1	Team spirit 2	Communication 3	Open-minded / understanding 4	Commitment 5	Swiftness 6	Honesty 7
experience	team work	regular interaction	willingness to compromise but do a superior job	finish job- bring to conclusion	swiftness, responsiveness	honesty
years of experience	team player	strong negotiation skills	cross cultural awareness	commited	pro-active	objective
quality of work	team player	communication skills (good, open, honest)	understanding different cultures	commitment	pro-activeness	honesty
competence in subject matter	team spirit	clear & precise interpersonal skills	respect for other team members	commitment to success	responsive	trust worthy
Competence	team spirit	communication skills	appreciation of good work of others	commited	reactive	honesty
Competences	team player	frequent communication CC, EM,	respect (even where everyone can contribute & give ideas)	strong commitment	responsiveness	honesty
Competence	excellent team spirit	open & frequent communication	understanding	dedication to work	swiftness of reaction (& respect of deadlines)	trustworthiness
Competent	friendly	communication skills	open mind	commitment to get the job done	pro-active attitude towards each team member	honesty
competences, skills in work	team welcoming	strong interpersonal skills	understanding	commitment	good time response	integrity
competences (1st class work)	think positive	communication skills	kindness	commited (one goal: the project's success, not one's personal success)	prompt replies	integrity of parties involved
1st class support & response	constructive attitude	Communication ability	understanding	commitment		loyalty
quality of the answer	constructive attitude	communication skills (emotional intelligence)	open-minded	active participation		modesty
quality of work (& confidentiality)	permanent enthusiasm (& envy to communicate)	regular communication set -up	open-minded, adaptive	direct & honest input		trust other team members until they prove otherwise
	pleasant personal disposition	communication	two-day answers			
answer every time	enthusiasm	discussion	consistency of other person's feeling			
accuracy	willingness to do what it takes	collaboration				
accuracy						
correct & valid information (on time)						
response to requirements						
meet commitments						
respect of the deadline						
punctuality						

Availability 8	Clear goals 9	Reliability 10	Flexibility 11	Responsibility 12	Rationality / anticipation 13	Leadership 14
availability	team scope	reliable	flexibility	willingness to accept responsibility	reasoning	strong personality
availability	common mission	reliable	flexibility	responsibility	rational thinker	leadership
availability	same objectives/goals	reliability	Flexibility	acceptance of blame (don't pretend it's blame on others)	not focus on people but on principles	
availability	clear roles & responsabilities	reliability	flexibility		level-headed	
availability	clear understanding of roles & duties	reliability	flexibility		forecasting	
availability	clear objectives	reliability	flexibility		consistency	
availability	correct formulation of objectives					
ability to assist						
willing to help						
exchange best practices infos						

Appendix 2b   CODING TAXONOMY for Q33 & Q34

Q33.

	1	2	3	4	5	6	7	8
1	FR	UK	USA	B	LUX	BRAZIL	JPN	D
2	FR	UK	USA	B	LUX	BRAZIL	JPN	NL
3	FR	UK	USA	B				Hungary
4	FR	UK	USA	B				Romania
5	FR	UK	USA	B				Turkey
6	FR	UK	USA					Italy
7	FR	UK	USA					KSA
8	FR	UK						Sweden
9	FR	UK						
10	FR	UK						
11	Fr	UK						
12	FR	UK						
13	FR	UK						
14	FR							
15	FR							
16	FR							
17	FR							

Q34.

	1	2	3	4	5	6	7	8
1	FR	UK	USA	B	-	-	-	D
2	FR							CH
								EU

Appendix 2c   CODING TAXONOMY for Q39

Q39. Can you state your 3 preferred hobbies?

1	2	3	4	5	6	7	8
Sports	Travel	Reading	Music	Movies / Arts	Community	Nature	Miscellaneous
sports	travel	reading	music	Arts (movie, comcert, opera, theater)	my wife	nature	wine making
tennis	tourism	books	drums	cinema	family	nature	food
tennis	travelling	books	listening to music	movies	friends	gardening	cooking
long distance treck	travel	books	playing guitar	the arts	friends	gardening	cooking
swim	sightseeing	books	music	cartoons	friends		stamp collection
hiking	travel	reading	music	movies	friends		geneology
Horse back riding	camping	reading	dance	movies	socialising		antiques
vtt	beach	reading	music	movies	socialising		trading
outdoor sports	travel	reading	dance	cinema	pub		world affairs
golf	travel	reading	listen to classical music	cinema	restaurants		work
tennis	travel	reading	hi-fi	cinema	shopping		computers
ski	travel	reading	music				games
sports	travel	reading	latin american dancing				
sport	travel	reading					
golf	travel	reading					
cricket	travel	reading					
walking	travel	reading					
swimming	travel	reading					
bike riding	travel						
aerobics	travel						
hiking	travel						
yoga	travel						
sports							
soccer							
bike riding							
sport							
driving							
sport							
ski							
ski							
golf							
yoga							
gym							
motocross							
horse-riding							
karate							
ski							
sport							
water sports							
ski							
cycling							
soccer							
ice-hockey							
sports							
off shore fishing							
running							
aerobics							

Appendix 3

TYPOLOGY of SURVEY QUESTIONS

1.   BELIEF data

What the respondant THINK or BELIEVE about something

E.g.
• In general, « do financial advisors place their clients' interests before their own ? »

☐ Always yes
☐ Usually yes
☐ Sometimes yes
☐ Seldom yes
☐ Never yes

• Please describe what you think would be the main impact on employees of a nil hours contract ?

2.   ATTITUDE data

How the respondant FEELs about something

E.g.
• How do you feel about the following statement ? «…»
• Do you agree or disagree with the use of nil hours contracts by employers ?

3.   ATTRIBUTE data

Question about the CHARACTERISTICS of the respondant

E.g.
What is your marital status ?

☐ Single
☐ Married

☐ Divorced
☐ Other

4.   BEHAVIOR data

Question about the CONCRETE EXPERIENCE of the respondant.

E.g.
• Have you ever been employed on a nil hours contract ?

☐ Yes
☐ No
☐ Not sure

• How often do you place your clients' interests before your own ?

☐ 80-100 % of my time
☐ 60-70 % of my time
☐ 40-59 % of my time
☐ 20-39 % of my time
☐ 0-19 % of my time

Source: Saunders *et al*

Appendix 4

Recruitements of the Candidates (for the survey)

Appendix 4a

1. First e-mail:

PERSONAL MATTERS

Good morning (name) !

It would be very kind of you if you could do me a favour with regards to the following matter:

Currently working on his thesis linked to the award of an MBA degree, Olivier Chavaren is now conducting a survey on Trust which is part of a research project to facilitate a better understanding of how Trust in Global Virtual Teams (i.e. within non-collocated teams around the world) emerges and can be sustained over time. A more precise definition of a Virtual Team is provided at the end of this document. The survey should not take you more than 15-20 minutes to fill in. The questionnaire is anonymous and you cannot be identified from the information you provide. The aim is to analyze data as a whole only to attempt to capture a trend.

Could you please provide me with 5 (or more) e-mail addresses of people (preferably executives) you know who would be keen on answering the survey. Obviously, these people must work with other remote colleagues through e-mail, telephone or videoconferencing.

We hope that you will find completing the questionnaire enjoyable, and thank you in advance for helping us. Should you have any queries or would like further information about this project, please call me on +44 01256 XXX XXX.
Thank you for your help.

Have a nice day !

Best regards

Sender's name.
NB: what is a Global Virtual Team?
„A global virtual team is an example of a new organization form, where a temporary team is assembled on an as-needed basis for the duration of a task, and staffed by members from the far comers of the world. In such a team, members physically remain on different continents and in different countries, interact primarily through the use of computer-mediated communication technologies (electronic mail, telephone or even videoconferencing, etc.), and rarely or never see each other in person.„

Appendix 4b

2nd e-mail
Cover letter for the questionnaire

(sent by e-mail from trust-in-global-virtual-teams@voila.fr)

Dear (name)

This survey is part of a research project to understand better how *Trust in Global Virtual Teams* (i.e. within non-collocated teams around the world) emerges and can be sustained over time. A more precise definition of this concept is provided at the end of this document. This study will be assessed as part of the award of my MBA degree.

Please answer the questions freely. The questionnaire is <u>fully anonymous</u> (as we are using an 'Anonymiser' that removes the 'From' field) and you cannot be identified from the information you provide. As soon as you have filled in the questionnaire, the data will be entered automatically in an ad hoc software and processed as a whole. Therefore, we have no access to the completed individual respondent's form.

ALL THE INFORMATION YOU PROVIDE WILL BE TREATED IN
THE STRICTEST CONFIDENCE

The questionnaire should not take you more than 15-20 minutes to complete. Please answer the questions in the space provided. Try to complete the questions at a time you are unlikely to be disturbed. Also, do not spend too long on any one question. Your first thoughts are usually the best!

Even if you feel the items covered may not apply directly to you in your relationship with trust please do not ignore them. Your answers are essential in building an accurate picture of what people find important when embarking on a trust behaviour.

WHEN YOU HAVE COMPLETED THE QUESTIONNAIRE (deadline: 5th Sept.), PLEASE
SAVE IT on your hard disk
1. Then E-MAIL IT AS AN ATTACHMENT to anonymous@mail.rhbnc.ac.uk
2. With 'survey' as subject (without any personal signature or name in the text field)

We hope that you find completing the questionnaire enjoyable, and thank you for taking the time to help us. Should you have any queries or would like further information about this project, please call me on +44 1256 468 310.

Thank you for your help.
Yours sincerely

Olivier CHAVAREN
MBA Student / University of London
Royal Holloway/ School of Management

NB:
1. What is a *Global Virtual Team*?
"It is team where members physically remain on different continents and in different countries, interact primarily through the use of computer-mediated communication technologies (electronic mail, telephone or even videoconferencing, etc.), and rarely or never see each other in person. „

2. To qualify for the survey, it is important that you fulfil at least the 2 following criteria:
     - working mainly through e-mail, telephone/conference call or videoconference
     - with colleagues in different places.

Appendix 4c

Follow-up letter (sent by e-mail from trust-in-global-virtual-teams@voila.fr)

Dear (name),

We have already received many responses for the survey regarding Trust in Global Virtual Teams. Many thanks for your assistance.

However, we did not receive ALL the responses yet. We would appreciate if you could check that your answers have been sent. If not, you can still send it to: anonymous@mail.rhbnc.ac.uk

Moreover, some respondents mentioned that they need the survey in XL 95 version. Therefore, both versions are attached below.

If you have already responded to the survey, PLEASE disregard this letter.

Thanks again.

Olivier

Appendix 5

Frequency Table

q3 to q12: testing the propositions

1 means the respondant disagrees very strongly and 10 he agrees very strongly.

Q3: In a virtual team, the perception of my colleagues' trustworthiness/confidence is influenced by 'institutionals factors'

		Frequency	Percent	Valid Percent	Cumulative Percent
Valid	1.00	3	5.5	5.5	5.5
	2.00	3	5.5	5.5	10.9
	3.00	5	9.1	9.1	20.0
	4.00	9	16.4	16.4	36.4
	5.00	9	16.4	16.4	52.7
	6.00	8	14.5	14.5	67.3
	7.00	6	10.9	10.9	78.2
	8.00	5	9.1	9.1	87.3
	9.00	5	9.1	9.1	96.4
	10.00	2	3.6	3.6	100.0
	Total	55	100.0	100.0	

Q4: In a virtual team, in order to achieve my working goals, I depend very much on other colleagues

		Frequency	Percent	Valid Percent	Cumulative Percent
Valid	1.00	1	1.8	1.8	1.8
	2.00	1	1.8	1.8	3.6
	4.00	5	9.1	9.1	12.7
	5.00	2	3.6	3.6	16.4
	6.00	9	16.4	16.4	32.7
	7.00	5	9.1	9.1	41.8
	8.00	10	18.2	18.2	60.0
	9.00	13	23.6	23.6	83.6
	10.00	9	16.4	16.4	100.0
	Total	55	100.0	100.0	

Q5: In a virtual team, I usually concentrate on action as soon as possible (i.e. 'swift trust') instead of focusing on social exchanges.

		Frequency	Percent	Valid Percent	Cumulative Percent
Valid	1.00	1	1.8	1.8	1.8
	3.00	1	1.8	1.8	3.6
	4.00	3	5.5	5.5	9.1
	5.00	10	18.2	18.2	27.3
	6.00	12	21.8	21.8	49.1
	7.00	6	10.9	10.9	60.0
	8.00	6	10.9	10.9	70.9
	9.00	10	18.2	18.2	89.1
	10.00	6	10.9	10.9	100.0
	Total	55	100.0	100.0	

Q6: In a virtual team, I usually believe that my team partners are competent

		Frequency	Percent	Valid Percent	Cumulativ e Percent
Valid	1.00	2	3.6	3.6	3.6
	3.00	2	3.6	3.6	7.3
	4.00	3	5.5	5.5	12.7
	5.00	7	12.7	12.7	25.5
	6.00	8	14.5	14.5	40.0
	7.00	7	12.7	12.7	52.7
	8.00	13	23.6	23.6	76.4
	9.00	11	20.0	20.0	96.4
	10.00	2	3.6	3.6	100.0
	Total	55	100.0	100.0	

Q7: In a virtual team, I usually believe that my team partners have a good level of 'interpersonal skills'.

		Frequency	Percent	Valid Percent	Cumulativ e Percent
Valid	1.00	1	1.8	1.8	1.8
	3.00	1	1.8	1.8	3.6
	4.00	7	12.7	12.7	16.4
	5.00	9	16.4	16.4	32.7
	6.00	11	20.0	20.0	52.7
	7.00	6	10.9	10.9	63.6
	8.00	10	18.2	18.2	81.8
	9.00	6	10.9	10.9	92.7
	10.00	4	7.3	7.3	100.0
	Total	55	100.0	100.0	

Q8: In a virtual team, I believe my team partners think and act like I do when it comes to concrete things.

		Frequency	Percent	Valid Percent	Cumulativ e Percent
Valid	1.00	4	7.3	7.3	7.3
	2.00	3	5.5	5.5	12.7
	3.00	8	14.5	14.5	27.3
	4.00	7	12.7	12.7	40.0
	5.00	10	18.2	18.2	58.2
	6.00	6	10.9	10.9	69.1
	7.00	8	14.5	14.5	83.6
	8.00	3	5.5	5.5	89.1
	9.00	4	7.3	7.3	96.4
	10.00	2	3.6	3.6	100.0
	Total	55	100.0	100.0	

Q9: In a virtual team, I find it easy to predict the action of my 'virtual' colleagues

		Frequency	Percent	Valid Percent	Cumulativ e Percent
Valid	1.00	2	3.6	3.6	3.6
	2.00	6	10.9	10.9	14.5
	3.00	10	18.2	18.2	32.7
	4.00	8	14.5	14.5	47.3
	5.00	11	20.0	20.0	67.3
	6.00	7	12.7	12.7	80.0
	7.00	1	1.8	1.8	81.8
	8.00	3	5.5	5.5	87.3
	9.00	5	9.1	9.1	96.4
	10.00	2	3.6	3.6	100.0
	Total	55	100.0	100.0	

Q10: In a virtual team, I believe my team partners display good will when interacting with each other.

		Frequency	Percent	Valid Percent	Cumulativ e Percent
Valid	1.00	1	1.8	1.8	1.8
	3.00	3	5.5	5.5	7.3
	5.00	11	20.0	20.0	27.3
	6.00	9	16.4	16.4	43.6
	7.00	9	16.4	16.4	60.0
	8.00	10	18.2	18.2	78.2
	9.00	8	14.5	14.5	92.7
	10.00	4	7.3	7.3	100.0
	Total	55	100.0	100.0	

Q11: In a virtual team, I can easily absorb some occasional acts of mistrust by others

		Frequency	Percent	Valid Percent	Cumulativ e Percent
Valid	.00	1	1.8	1.8	1.8
	1.00	5	9.1	9.1	10.9
	2.00	3	5.5	5.5	16.4
	3.00	12	21.8	21.8	38.2
	4.00	12	21.8	21.8	60.0
	5.00	8	14.5	14.5	74.5
	6.00	5	9.1	9.1	83.6
	7.00	3	5.5	5.5	89.1
	8.00	2	3.6	3.6	92.7
	9.00	4	7.3	7.3	100.0
	Total	55	100.0	100.0	

Q12: In a virtual team, when relationships are strong and reliable, I believe trust may transfer from one person to another (through reputation effect).

		Frequency	Percent	Valid Percent	Cumulativ e Percent
Valid	1.00	2	3.6	3.6	3.6
	3.00	3	5.5	5.5	9.1
	4.00	2	3.6	3.6	12.7
	5.00	3	5.5	5.5	18.2
	6.00	9	16.4	16.4	34.5
	7.00	9	16.4	16.4	50.9
	8.00	7	12.7	12.7	63.6
	9.00	11	20.0	20.0	83.6
	10.00	9	16.4	16.4	100.0
	Total	55	100.0	100.0	

Histogram

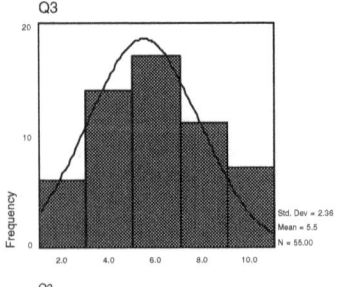

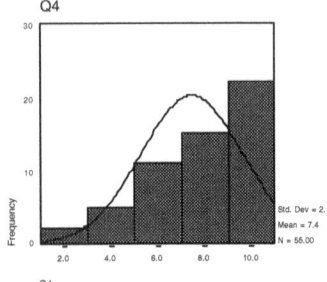

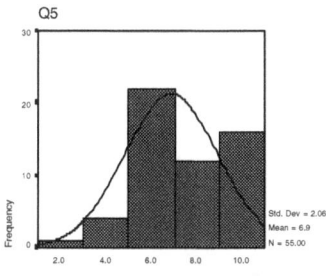

Q5

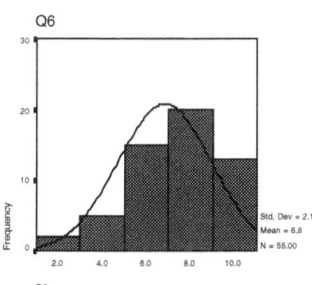

Q6

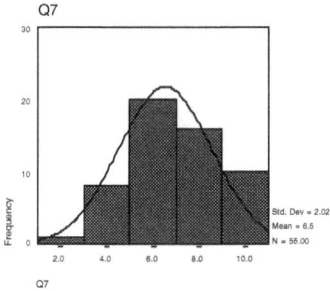

Q7

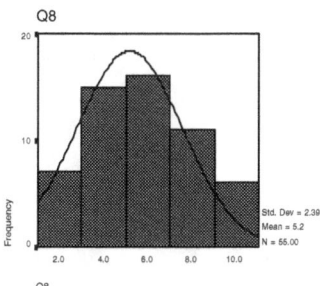

Q8

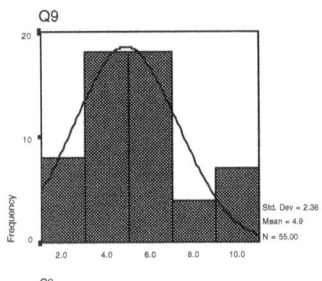

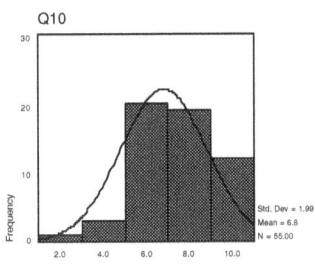

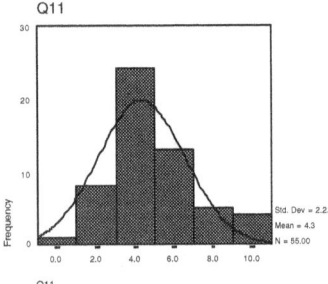

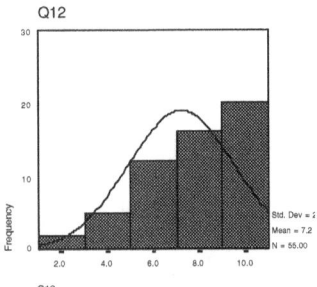

Appendix 5b

Frequencies

Statistics

		Q2A	Q2B	Q2C
N	Valid	50	50	50
	Missing	0	0	0

Frequency Table

Q2A

		Frequency	Percent	Valid Percent	Cumulative Percent
Valid	2	1	2.0	2.0	2.0
	4	5	10.0	10.0	12.0
	5	5	10.0	10.0	22.0
	6	35	70.0	70.0	92.0
	7	3	6.0	6.0	98.0
	8	1	2.0	2.0	100.0
	Total	50	100.0	100.0	

Q2B

		Frequency	Percent	Valid Percent	Cumulative Percent
Valid	.00	1	2.0	2.0	2.0
	2.00	5	10.0	10.0	12.0
	3.00	3	6.0	6.0	18.0
	4.00	8	16.0	16.0	34.0
	5.00	10	20.0	20.0	54.0
	6.00	9	18.0	18.0	72.0
	7.00	6	12.0	12.0	84.0
	8.00	6	12.0	12.0	96.0
	9.00	2	4.0	4.0	100.0
	Total	50	100.0	100.0	

Q2C

		Frequency	Percent	Valid Percent	Cumulative Percent
Valid	.00	1	2.0	2.0	2.0
	1.00	6	12.0	12.0	14.0
	2.00	5	10.0	10.0	24.0
	3.00	3	6.0	6.0	30.0
	4.00	11	22.0	22.0	52.0
	5.00	6	12.0	12.0	64.0
	6.00	2	4.0	4.0	68.0
	7.00	4	8.0	8.0	76.0
	8.00	10	20.0	20.0	96.0
	9.00	2	4.0	4.0	100.0
	Total	50	100.0	100.0	

Histogram

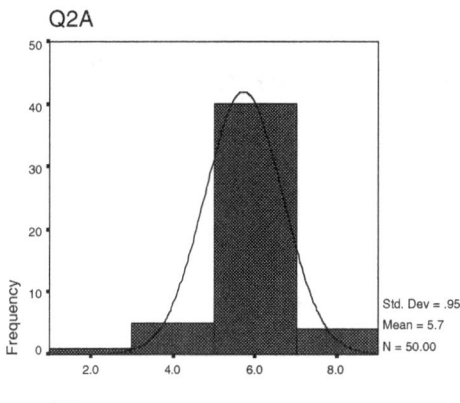

Q2A

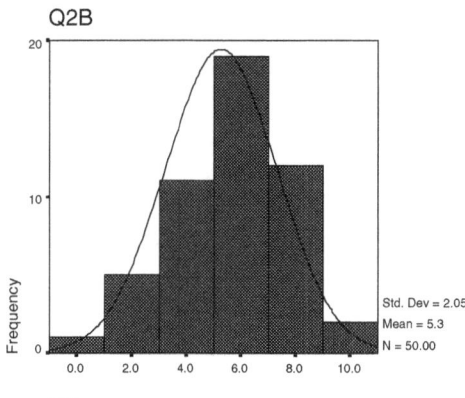

Q2B

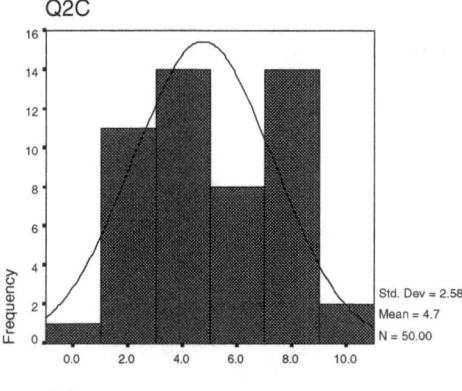

Q2C

Appendix 5c

Frequencies: question 1: has trust declined generally speaking?

Q1A : State

		Frequency	Percent	Valid Percent	Cumulativ e Percent
Valid	1 (-)	23	46.0	46.0	46.0
	2 (=)	21	42.0	42.0	88.0
	3 (+)	6	12.0	12.0	100.0
	Total	50	100.0	100.0	

Q1B: Legal system

		Frequency	Percent	Valid Percent	Cumulativ e Percent
Valid	1	21	42.0	42.0	42.0
	2	25	50.0	50.0	92.0
	3	4	8.0	8.0	100.0
	Total	50	100.0	100.0	

Q1C: Police

		Frequency	Percent	Valid Percent	Cumulativ e Percent
Valid	1.00	24	48.0	48.0	48.0
	2.00	23	46.0	46.0	94.0
	3.00	3	6.0	6.0	100.0
	Total	50	100.0	100.0	

Q1D: Work

		Frequency	Percent	Valid Percent	Cumulative Percent
Valid	1.00	5	10.0	10.0	10.0
	2.00	24	48.0	48.0	58.0
	3.00	21	42.0	42.0	100.0
	Total	50	100.0	100.0	

Q1E: Education

		Frequency	Percent	Valid Percent	Cumulative Percent
Valid	1.00	18	36.0	36.0	36.0
	2.00	13	26.0	26.0	62.0
	3.00	19	38.0	38.0	100.0
	Total	50	100.0	100.0	

Q1F: Family

		Frequency	Percent	Valid Percent	Cumulative Percent
Valid	1.00	6	12.0	12.0	12.0
	2.00	13	26.0	26.0	38.0
	3.00	31	62.0	62.0	100.0
	Total	50	100.0	100.0	

Q1G: Religion

		Frequency	Percent	Valid Percent	Cumulative Percent
Valid	1.00	16	32.0	32.0	32.0
	2.00	24	48.0	48.0	80.0
	3.00	10	20.0	20.0	100.0
	Total	50	100.0	100.0	

Q1H: Culture

		Frequency	Percent	Valid Percent	Cumulative Percent
Valid	1.00	8	16.0	16.0	16.0
	2.00	24	48.0	48.0	64.0
	3.00	18	36.0	36.0	100.0
	Total	50	100.0	100.0	

Q1I: Sport

		Frequency	Percent	Valid Percent	Cumulative Percent
Valid	1.00	15	30.0	30.0	30.0
	2.00	20	40.0	40.0	70.0
	3.00	15	30.0	30.0	100.0
	Total	50	100.0	100.0	

Frequencies

Q1A

		Frequency	Percent	Valid Percent	Cumulativ e Percent
Valid	1	23	46.0	46.0	46.0
	2	21	42.0	42.0	88.0
	3	6	12.0	12.0	100.0
	Total	50	100.0	100.0	

Q1B

		Frequency	Percent	Valid Percent	Cumulativ e Percent
Valid	1	21	42.0	42.0	42.0
	2	25	50.0	50.0	92.0
	3	4	8.0	8.0	100.0
	Total	50	100.0	100.0	

Q1C

		Frequency	Percent	Valid Percent	Cumulativ e Percent
Valid	1.00	24	48.0	48.0	48.0
	2.00	23	46.0	46.0	94.0
	3.00	3	6.0	6.0	100.0
	Total	50	100.0	100.0	

Q1D

		Frequency	Percent	Valid Percent	Cumulativ e Percent
Valid	1.00	5	10.0	10.0	10.0
	2.00	24	48.0	48.0	58.0
	3.00	21	42.0	42.0	100.0
	Total	50	100.0	100.0	

Q1E

		Frequency	Percent	Valid Percent	Cumulativ e Percent
Valid	1.00	18	36.0	36.0	36.0
	2.00	13	26.0	26.0	62.0
	3.00	19	38.0	38.0	100.0
	Total	50	100.0	100.0	

Q1F

		Frequency	Percent	Valid Percent	Cumulativ e Percent
Valid	1.00	6	12.0	12.0	12.0
	2.00	13	26.0	26.0	38.0
	3.00	31	62.0	62.0	100.0
	Total	50	100.0	100.0	

Q1G

		Frequency	Percent	Valid Percent	Cumulativ e Percent
Valid	1.00	16	32.0	32.0	32.0
	2.00	24	48.0	48.0	80.0
	3.00	10	20.0	20.0	100.0
	Total	50	100.0	100.0	

Q1H

		Frequency	Percent	Valid Percent	Cumulativ e Percent
Valid	1.00	8	16.0	16.0	16.0
	2.00	24	48.0	48.0	64.0
	3.00	18	36.0	36.0	100.0
	Total	50	100.0	100.0	

Q1I

		Frequency	Percent	Valid Percent	Cumulativ e Percent
Valid	1.00	15	30.0	30.0	30.0
	2.00	20	40.0	40.0	70.0
	3.00	15	30.0	30.0	100.0
	Total	50	100.0	100.0	

Histogram

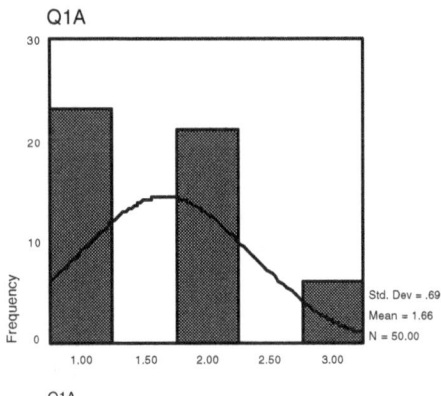

Q1A

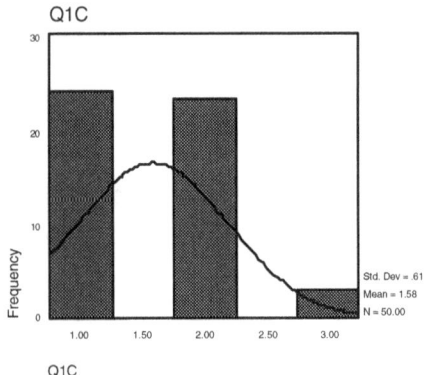

Q1C

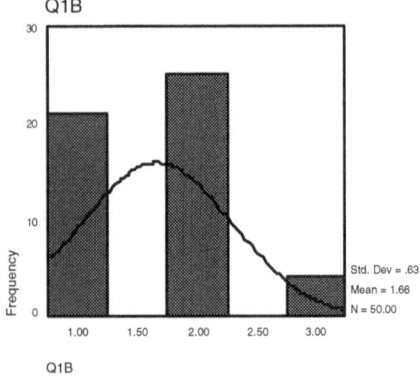

Q1B

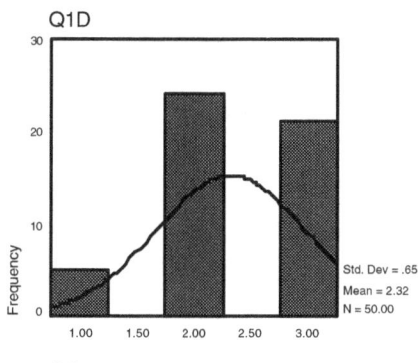

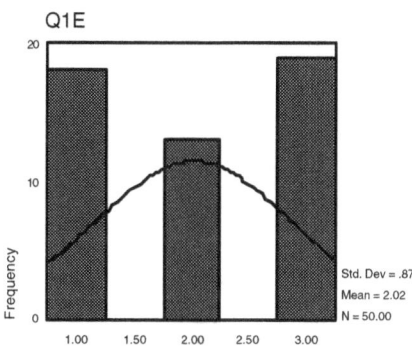

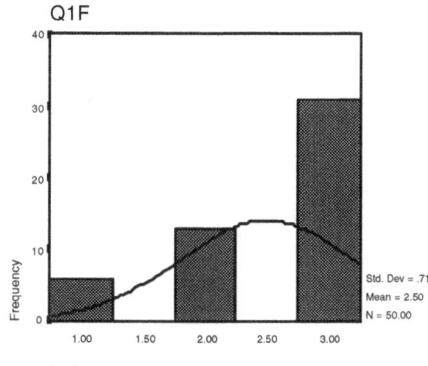

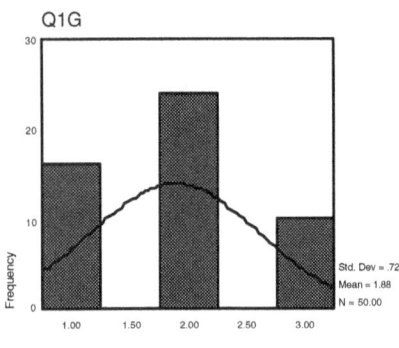

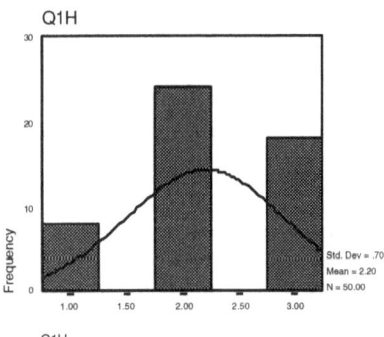

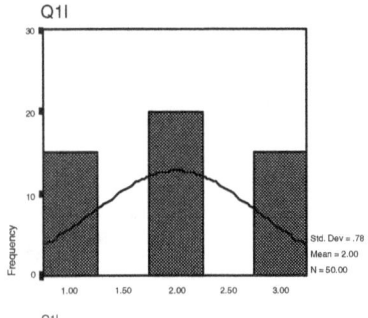

Appedix 6

Correlation Metrics

Descriptive Statistics

	Mean	Std. Deviation	N
Q3	5.4545	2.3556	55
Q4	7.4364	2.1753	55
Q5	6.8727	2.0643	55
Q6	6.8182	2.1090	55
Q7	6.5273	2.0171	55
Q8	5.1636	2.3864	55
Q9	4.8909	2.3623	55
Q10	6.8000	1.9851	55
Q11	4.3273	2.2199	55
Q12	7.2000	2.3126	55

Correlations

		Q3	Q4	Q5	Q6	Q7	Q8	Q9	Q10	Q11	Q12
Q3	Pearson Correlation	1.000	-.036	-.197	-.099	-.016	.033	.009	-.091	-.075	-.014
	Sig. (2-tailed)	.	.795	.149	.474	.906	.813	.948	.508	.586	.922
	Sum of Squares and Cross-products	299.6	-9.909	-51.818	-26.455	-4.182	9.909	2.727	-23.000	-21.182	-4.000
	Covariance	5.549	-.184	-.960	-.490	-.077	.184	5.1E-02	-.426	-.392	-.074
	N	55	55	55	55	55	55	55	55	55	55
Q4	Pearson Correlation	-.036	1.000	.272*	.098	.111	.328*	.053	.145	-.111	.200
	Sig. (2-tailed)	.795	.	.044	.475	.419	.014	.702	.291	.421	.144
	Sum of Squares and Cross-products	-9.909	255.527	66.055	24.364	26.345	92.073	14.618	33.800	-28.855	54.200
	Covariance	-.184	4.732	1.223	.451	.488	1.705	.271	.626	-.534	1.004
	N	55	55	55	55	55	55	55	55	55	55
Q5	Pearson Correlation	-.197	.272*	1.000	.326*	.265	.271*	.320*	.409**	.179	.362**
	Sig. (2-tailed)	.149	.044	.	.015	.050	.045	.017	.002	.191	.007
	Sum of Squares and Cross-products	-51.82	66.055	230.11	76.727	59.691	72.145	84.236	90.600	44.291	93.400
	Covariance	-.960	1.223	4.261	1.421	1.105	1.336	1.560	1.678	.820	1.730
	N	55	55	55	55	55	55	55	55	55	55
Q6	Pearson Correlation	-.099	.098	.326*	1.000	.641**	.459**	.356**	.464**	.120	.372**
	Sig. (2-tailed)	.474	.475	.015	.	.000	.000	.008	.000	.384	.005
	Sum of Squares and Cross-products	-26.45	24.364	76.727	240.182	147.273	124.636	95.909	105.00	30.273	98.000
	Covariance	-.490	.451	1.421	4.448	2.727	2.308	1.776	1.944	.561	1.815
	N	55	55	55	55	55	55	55	55	55	55
Q7	Pearson Correlation	-.016	.111	.265	.641**	1.000	.470**	.405**	.517**	.159	.299*
	Sig. (2-tailed)	.906	.419	.050	.000	.	.000	.002	.000	.245	.027
	Sum of Squares and Cross-products	-4.182	26.345	59.691	147.273	219.709	122.255	104.164	111.80	38.509	75.200
	Covariance	-.077	.488	1.105	2.727	4.069	2.264	1.929	2.070	.713	1.393
	N	55	55	55	55	55	55	55	55	55	55
Q8	Pearson Correlation	.033	.328*	.271*	.459**	.470**	1.000	.374**	.288*	.105	.259
	Sig. (2-tailed)	.813	.014	.045	.000	.000	.	.005	.033	.445	.056
	Sum of Squares and Cross-products	9.909	92.073	72.145	124.636	122.255	307.527	113.982	73.800	30.055	77.200
	Covariance	.184	1.705	1.336	2.308	2.264	5.695	2.111	1.367	.557	1.430
	N	55	55	55	55	55	55	55	55	55	55
Q9	Pearson Correlation	.009	.053	.320*	.356**	.405**	.374**	1.000	.252	.176	.096
	Sig. (2-tailed)	.948	.702	.017	.008	.002	.005	.	.064	.198	.488
	Sum of Squares and Cross-products	2.727	14.618	84.236	95.909	104.164	113.982	301.345	63.800	49.964	28.200
	Covariance	.051	.271	1.560	1.776	1.929	2.111	5.580	1.181	.925	.522
	N	55	55	55	55	55	55	55	55	55	55
Q10	Pearson Correlation	-.091	.145	.409**	.464**	.517**	.288*	.252	1.000	.011	.396**
	Sig. (2-tailed)	.508	.291	.002	.000	.000	.033	.064	.	.937	.003
	Sum of Squares and Cross-products	-23.00	33.800	90.600	105.000	111.800	73.800	63.800	212.80	2.600	98.200
	Covariance	-.426	.626	1.678	1.944	2.070	1.367	1.181	3.941	.048	1.819
	N	55	55	55	55	55	55	55	55	55	55
Q11	Pearson Correlation	-.075	-.111	.179	.120	.159	.105	.176	.011	1.000	.229
	Sig. (2-tailed)	.586	.421	.191	.384	.245	.445	.198	.937	.	.093
	Sum of Squares and Cross-products	-21.18	-28.855	44.291	30.273	38.509	30.055	49.964	2.600	266.11	63.400
	Covariance	-.392	-.534	.820	.561	.713	.557	.925	5.E-02	4.928	1.174
	N	55	55	55	55	55	55	55	55	55	55
Q12	Pearson Correlation	-.014	.200	.362**	.372**	.299*	.259	.096	.396**	.229	1.000
	Sig. (2-tailed)	.922	.144	.007	.005	.027	.056	.488	.003	.093	.
	Sum of Squares and Cross-products	-4.000	54.200	93.400	98.000	75.200	77.200	28.200	98.200	63.400	288.8
	Covariance	-.074	1.004	1.730	1.815	1.393	1.430	.522	1.819	1.174	5.348
	N	55	55	55	55	55	55	55	55	55	55

*. Correlation is significant at the 0.05 level (2-tailed).

**. Correlation is significant at the 0.01 level (2-tailed).

Appendix 7

Crosstabs: Q4 * Q24A

Q4.In a virtual team, in order to achieve my working goals, I depend very much on other colleagues.
Q24a. Number of e-mails received (per day)

Count

		| 1.00	2.00	4.00	5.00	7.00	10	12	13	15.0	20	25	30	35	40	45.0	50	60	70	75	100	120	Total
Q4	1.00																				1			1
	2.00				1																		1
	4.00			1	1		1						1		1								5
	5.00										1					1							2
	6.00	1					1			2			2		1						1	1	9
	7.00				1		2			2													5
	8.00						2			1	1	1	1		1			2	1				10
	9.00							1	1		1		2	2	2		1	1	1		1		13
	10.0		1			1					2	1	3				1						9
Total		1	1	1	3	1	6	1	1	5	5	2	9	2	5	1	2	3	2	1	2	1	55

Chi-Square Tests

	Value	df	Asymp. Sig. (2-sided)
Pearson Chi-Square	196.714[a]	160	.026
Likelihood Ratio	111.942	160	.999
Linear-by-Linear Association	.021	1	.885
N of Valid Cases	55		

a. 189 cells (100.0%) have expected count less than 5.
The minimum expected count is .02.

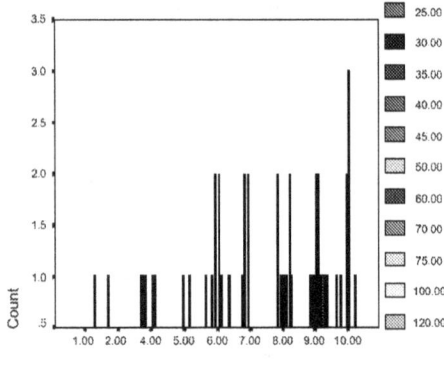

Appendix 8

Crosstabs:Q5 * Q24A

Q5. In a virtual team, I usually concentrate on action as soon as possible (i.e. 'swift trust') instead of focusing on socia
Q24a. Number of e-mails received (per day)

Count

		Q24A																					Total
		1.00	2.00	4.00	5.00	7.00	10	12	13	15	20	25	30	35	40	45	50	60	70	75	100	120	
Q5	1.00																			1			1
	3.00										1												1
	4.00																	1	1			1	3
	5.00				1		1			2		1	2		2						1		10
	6.00						2	1		2	1	1	2	1			1	1					12
	7.00				1								3		1				1				6
	8.00						1				2		1		1			1					6
	9.00			1	1		2			1	1		1	1	1	1							10
	10.00	1	1			1			1								1				1		6
Total		1	1	1	3	1	6	1	1	5	5	2	9	2	5	1	2	3	2	1	2	1	55

Chi-Square Tests

	Value	df	Asymp. Sig. (2-sided)
Pearson Chi-Square	189.169[a]	160	.057
Likelihood Ratio	110.362	160	.999
Linear-by-Linear Association	4.666	1	.031
N of Valid Cases	55		

a. 189 cells (100.0%) have expected count less than 5.
The minimum expected count is .02.

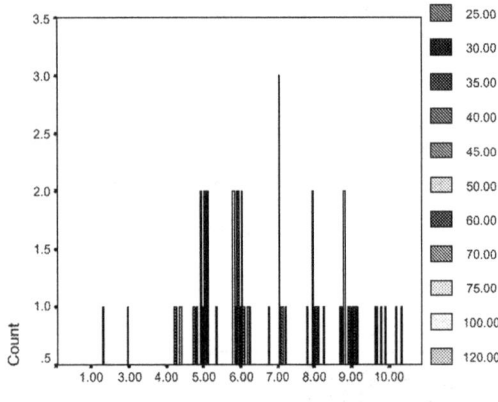

Q5

Q7 * Q24A

Q7. In a virtual team, I usually believe that my team partners have a good level of 'interpersonal skills'.
24A. Number of e-mails received (per day)

Count

		Q24A																					Total
		1.00	2.00	4.00	5.00	7.00	10	12	13	15	20	25	30	35	40	45	50	60	70	75	100	120	
Q7	1.00																			1			1
	3.00				1																		1
	4.00						1	1					3				1					1	7
	5.00						1			3					2	1			1		1		9
	6.00	1	1				1			1	1	1	3		1			1					11
	7.00								1		1		1	1	1				1				6
	8.00				1	1	1				1	1	2				1	2					10
	9.00			1	1		1				1				1						1		6
	10.00						1			1	1			1									4
Total		1	1	1	3	1	6	1	1	5	5	2	9	2	5	1	2	3	2	1	2	1	55

Chi-Square Tests

	Value	df	Asymp. Sig. (2-sided)
Pearson Chi-Square	183.585[a]	160	.098
Likelihood Ratio	112.828	160	.998
Linear-by-Linear Association	2.118	1	.146
N of Valid Cases	55		

a. 189 cells (100.0%) have expected count less than 5.
The minimum expected count is .02.

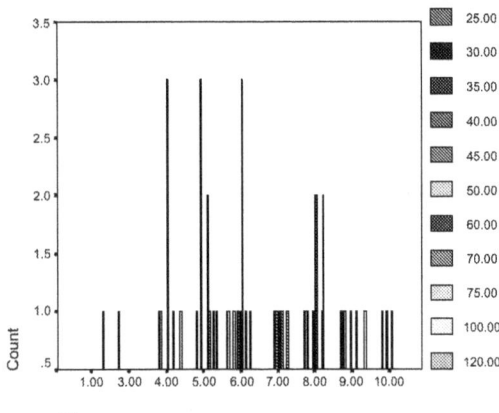

Crosstabs:Q9 * Q24A

Q9. In a virtual team, I find it easy to predict the action of my 'virtual' colleagues.
24A. Number of e-mails received (per day)

Count

		Q24A																					Total
		1.00	2.00	4.00	5.00	7.00	10	12.0	13	15	20	25	30	35	40	45	50	60	70	75	100	120	
Q9	1.00		1																	1			2
	2.00												1		1			1	2		1		6
	3.00				1		2			1		1	3		1							1	10
	4.00									3	1		1		1			1	1				8
	5.00	1					3			1	1		3				1	1					11
	6.00				1		1		1	1	1				1				1				7
	7.00												1										1
	8.00			1	1	1																	3
	9.00							1		1				2							1		5
	10.00									1					1								2
Total		1	1	1	3	1	6	1	1	5	5	2	9	2	5	1	2	3	2	1	2	1	55

Chi-Square Tests

	Value	df	Asymp. Sig. (2-sided)
Pearson Chi-Square	220.957[a]	180	.020
Likelihood Ratio	130.059	180	.998
Linear-by-Linear Association	2.495	1	.114
N of Valid Cases	55		

a. 210 cells (100.0%) have expected count less than 5.
The minimum expected count is .02.

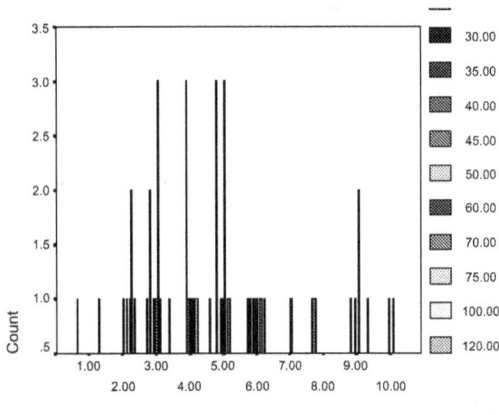

Q9

Crosstabs:Q10 * Q24A

Q10. In a virtual team, I believe my team partners display good will when interacting with each other.
24A. Number of e-mails received (per day)

Count

		Q24A																					Total
		1.00	2.00	4.00	5.00	7.00	10	12	13	15	20	25	30	35	40	45	50	60	70	75	100	120	
Q10	1.00																			1			1
	3.00												1					1			1		3
	5.00				1		1			2	1		1	1	2				1			1	11
	6.00							1		1	2		2		1			2					9
	7.00			1	1				1		2	1	2		1								9
	8.00					1	3			1		1	2			1	1						10
	9.00		1		1		2						1		1		1		1				8
	10.00	1								1				1							1		4
Total		1	1	1	3	1	6	1	1	5	5	2	9	2	5	1	2	3	2	1	2	1	55

Chi-Square Tests

	Value	df	Asymp. Sig. (2-sided)
Pearson Chi-Square	171.129[a]	140	.038
Likelihood Ratio	107.112	140	.982
Linear-by-Linear Association	4.772	1	.029
N of Valid Cases	55		

a. 168 cells (100.0%) have expected count less than 5. The minimum expected count is .02.

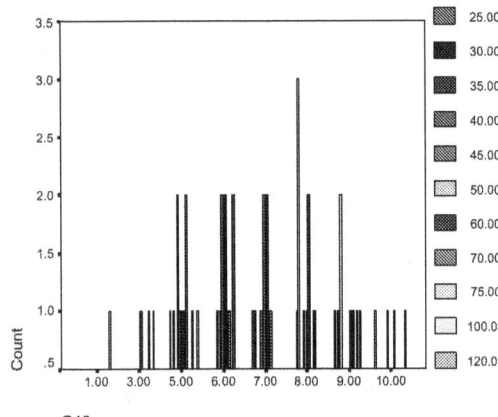

Q10

Crosstabs: Q11 * Q24A

Q11. In a virtual team, I can easily absorb some occasional acts of mistrust by others.
24A. Number of e-mails received (per day)

Count

		Q24A																					Total
		1.00	2.00	4.00	5.00	7.00	10.0	12	13	15	20	25	30	35	40	45	50	60	70	75	100	120	
Q11	.00																					1	1
	1.00							1							1		1	1	1				5
	2.00						1			1			1										3
	3.00		1	1	1					1			3	2	1	1		1					12
	4.00				1		3			1	1	1	3					1			1		12
	5.00	1					1		1		1		1		1				1	1			8
	6.00									1	2		1		1								5
	7.00						1					1					1						3
	8.00				1		1																2
	9.00				1						1				1						1		4
Total		1	1	1	3	1	6	1	1	5	5	2	9	2	5	1	2	3	2	1	2	1	55

Chi-Square Tests

	Value	df	Asymp. Sig. (2-sided)
Pearson Chi-Square	209.998[a]	180	.062
Likelihood Ratio	117.965	180	1.000
Linear-by-Linear Association	1.627	1	.202
N of Valid Cases	55		

a. 210 cells (100.0%) have expected count less than 5. The minimum expected count is .02.

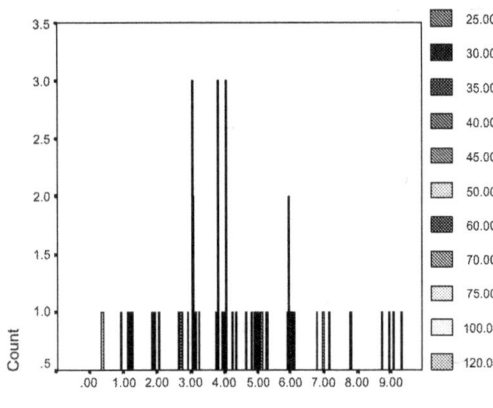

Q11

Appendix 13

Crosstabs: Q12 * Q24E

Q12. In a virtual team, when relationships are strong and reliable, I believe trust may transfer from one person to anot... (through reputation effect)
24E. Number of conference-calls (per month)

Count

		Q24E														Total
		.00	.50	1.00	2.00	3.00	4.00	5.00	6.00	8.00	10	12	15	20	25	
Q12	1.00						1						1			2
	3.00	1					1		1							3
	4.00						1					1				2
	5.00	1				1								1		3
	6.00	1			1	1	1	2			1		1		1	9
	7.00		1	1		4	1	2								9
	8.00				2	2	1			2						7
	9.00	3		2	2		3				1					11
	10.00	2		1		1		2		1	2					9
Total		8	1	3	6	8	10	6	1	3	4	1	2	1	1	55

Chi-Square Tests

	Value	df	Asymp. Sig. (2-sided)
Pearson Chi-Square	138.817[a]	104	.013
Likelihood Ratio	92.789	104	.777
Linear-by-Linear Association	3.177	1	.075
N of Valid Cases	55		

a. 126 cells (100.0%) have expected count less than 5. The minimum expected count is .04.

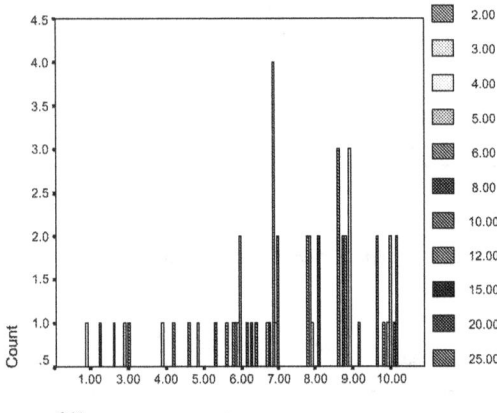

Q12

0-595-27577-X

www.ingramcontent.com/pod-product-compliance
Lightning Source LLC
Chambersburg PA
CBHW081152180526
45170CB00006B/2050